Instant Marketing for Almost Free

EFFECTIVE, LOW-COST RESULTS
IN WEEKS, DAYS OR HOURS

SUSAN F. BENJAMIN

SOURCEBOOKS, INC.
NAPERVILLE, ILLINOIS

Published by Sourcebooks, Inc.
P.O. Box 4410, Naperville, Illinois 60567-4410
(630) 961-3900
Fax: (630) 961-2168
www.sourcebooks.com

Library of Congress Cataloging-in-Publication Data
Benjamin, Susan
Instant marketing for almost free : effective, low-cost results in weeks, days, or hours / Susan F. Benjamin.
    p. cm.
Includes index.
ISBN-13: 978-1-4022-0824-9
ISBN-10: 1-4022-0824-3
1. Marketing. I. Title.
HF5415.B4292 2006
658.8—dc22
2006022428

Printed and bound in the United States of America.
SB 10 9 8 7 6 5 4 3 2 1

Contents

Introduction

Dr. Benjamin Spock, the noted pediatrician, once told parents, "You know more than you think you do." Well, the same holds true for marketing; actually, it probably holds truer, as you know if you've ever had kids. And if you've had the courage, ingenuity, and creativity to start a small business, or to get deeply involved with one, marketing should be a snap.

Your guiding principle will be the concept of marketing from within. That means to trust your gut. Break the rules. And value your own ideas above all else. First, though, you need to understand the core concepts of marketing—always know the rules before you break them. What has worked for other people? Why have certain marketing efforts failed? And how much money should you sink into your efforts? Here's what you can expect from this guide:

Section I: Getting Started

"Getting started" starts with you and your business. I'm speaking, of course, of one of the most essential (and mismanaged) components of marketing: your brand. That's why you'll step back and take a keen look. What is your brand? How does it distinguish you from the guy a few blocks down the road? And who are your customers? I mean, you *know* your customers, but are they really the right ones for you?

In more concrete terms, you'll identify core words, strategies, and images—from your logo to your business culture—that customers will equate with something compelling, desirable, and good. By the time you turn to Section II, you'll be ready to launch a powerful marketing campaign that is distinctly (and competitively) yours.

Section II: Marketing Imperatives

You know that developing marketing material requires skill. And knowledge. But everything from that first paragraph in your direct mail piece to the central image in your ad also requires strategy. You'll fuel your strategic power with the two chapters here, covering everything from the ten imperatives of marketing to facts about getting the right response from customers. No question—these will surprise you. In fact, the way you communicate at work may never be the same.

Section III: The Instant Marketing Supply Kit

Now, get ready to create the most important marketing supplies, from a brochure (that people actually read!) to your website, the great god of marketing today. Television ads, radio spots, telephone sales campaigns? Yes, we'll cover those, too. In fact, we'll address more marketing supplies than you'd imagine.

By the way, if that thought makes you panic—after all, you have only so much money and energy to devote to marketing—relax. We'll candidly discuss what items to put high or your priority list and which to wedge somewhere toward the bottom (website up, advertising down). If you want *everything*, and you want it *now*, still no problem. You'll get countless options for all your supplies—from the almost free or entirely free to the costly; from the do-it-yourself to hiring out. When you're finished, you'll have everything you need to make an instant marketing impression *and* keep your cash flow, well, flowing.

Section IV: People, Places, and Things: The Ultimate Marketing

Perhaps there's no greater instant marketing message than your window, your sign, or your personal presence. In this section, you'll get the nuts and bolts (and lobbies and displays) to do it right—and make a powerful statement instantly. Naturally, we'll cover the familiar, such as how to design the workplace to match your look with your brand. But we'll also cover the unfamiliar, such as establishing yourself as an expert by teaching adult education courses, or making a statement by turning your entryway into a museum (seriously, it's been done!). Some of these marketing devices are better than almost free—they actually pay!

Once you finish this book, don't pass it on to a friend (unless they promise to give it back) or stash it away. Keep it on your shelf, close by, where you can reach it. Why? Because marketing never ends. You should always be trying new ideas and adjusting the old ones, taking calculated risks and sometimes taking outrageous chances. But why talk here? Turn the page, and let's get going.

Section I.

Getting Started

Chapter 1

Taking the Mystery out of Marketing

Most people consider marketing a mysterious process that only professional marketers can master. Not so! Marketing is something you do every day. Think about it: most likely you talked to plenty of people about your business just yesterday or even today. Maybe you told them a funny story, or described your clients. Maybe you bragged a little about how great your product or service really is. Guess what? You were marketing.

Ten Cardinal Rules of Instant Marketing

The idea behind both formal marketing and informal chatting is simply that marketing maximizes the number of people who learn about your business. And the two most important tenets of any and all marketing are simple: convey the most appropriate and consistent image every time, and waste as little time, energy, and money as possible in getting the word out about your fabulous business. To start, let's look at the Ten Cardinal Rules of Instant Marketing. You'll apply these rules throughout this book—and for the rest of your marketing life. It's imperative that you remember these rules. Plenty of people forget them and regret it later—often sacrificing everything from thousands of dollars to the well-being of their businesses.

Who are you really selling to?

When marketing, you're trying to get someone to purchase your product or service. But what should we call that person? A prospect? A potential customer? Or how about a target? In this book, we're going to use the word customer, whether you're currently getting business from him or not. It's important to remember why—the reason should dictate much of your marketing approach:

• No matter what you're offering, you'll have better luck selling to existing customers than new ones. So factor them into your marketing plan as you move ahead.

• Much of your new business will come via word of mouth, thanks to existing customers. If they're happy, they'll send others to your door.

• A person or business can shift from being a prospect to a customer unexpectedly—and potentially years down the pike. That's because "no" often means "not yet." So even that prospect you're ready to write off could call up with a big-time contract.

1. Always take the Gumby approach to marketing

Remember Gumby? He was the endlessly bendable, green, doughlike figurine—a favorite toy for kids with a predilection for breaking things. Can't break Gumby! Unless you had a dog who liked to chew things, you had a hard time even denting him. Yet Gumby still had a form: two arms and legs and a single sweep of a torso. An odd form, and not what you'd call anatomically correct, but a form nonetheless.

Think of your marketing approach as a hard-hitting Gumby. You must give it form—the most compelling aspect of your product or service—depending on the people you want to reach and your competitors' marketing efforts. Yet your approach must be flexible as circumstances, opportunities, and market conditions appear, disappear, and evolve. And above all, your approach must be durable—able to withstand the upheaval every small business experiences.

2. Calculate the free, almost-free, in-debt, and pay-as-you-go finances of marketing

How you spend your marketing money is entirely your choice. You can invest hundreds of thousands of dollars, or do most of it for almost—even *altogether*—free. Yet some principles should be factored into your calculation. One is that you should go with freebies whenever possible, especially to test the more high-priced options. For example, when you put up your website, start with free hosting sites and see what works and what doesn't, then find one that charges a fee. Second, beware of going into debt for your marketing efforts. In fact, there are so many low-cost options that I say avoid debt completely. Third, generally avoid rental or monthly payment options aside from necessary expenses like rent. Slow cash flow is the nemesis of every small business, and you don't want to add unnecessary hardship. Finally, find unusual ways to judge just how well your marketing efforts work. There's a saying: "Marketing isn't expensive if it brings in lots of money." That's true, but how much money your marketing efforts yield can be a mystery answered only by time. See rule number 3!

3. Consider the instant *and* long-term marketing rewards

Some of your instant marketing *will* bring instant results—in weeks, days, even minutes—including big sales or contracts that last for years. But marketing can resemble growing a garden. You can't drop a seed in the ground and get a plant full of ripe tomatoes the next day. You have to wait weeks as the shoot springs from the ground, the plant grows, and it finally bears fruit.

Same thing with marketing. Sometimes your efforts will take months, even years, before bringing you a new customer. This partly explains why experts say the average business takes a good three years to become profitable. Your customer needs to know you, trust you, and depend on your offering. So don't think your marketing effort or business concept isn't working just because work isn't immediately gushing in! For example, years back, my marketing assistant called a large insurance company about a training course I was offering. The company was interested, so I went in, had a meeting with one of their vice presidents, and left. Everyone seemed happy . . . except I didn't hear from them. Until three years later, that is, when the VP called, saying the head of the department wanted to train his employees. She remembered our talk and pulled my card out of her Rolodex. I went back the next week and launched a relationship that has lasted fifteen years!

4. Remember, bigger isn't always better

Perhaps every business owner's marketing dream is to land a spot on *Oprah*, or to be interviewed on CNN. Even if you have a business selling house paints, you might be aching to sit on that studio chair and discuss how to blend colors. But remember, casting a broad net and reaching millions of people may not be as beneficial as a single cold call or a really great sign in front of your shop. Here's another story from my personal file. Several years ago, I was a guest on CNNfn. I was thrilled to do it, and when I was finished, everyone—the host, the camera crew, *everyone*—agreed the interview went well. They even rebroadcast it many times. A business owner's dream? Sure, except the television spot didn't directly generate any business. The cold calls my employee was making back at the office? That's a different—and more lucrative—story.

5. Stack your marketing efforts

No marketing effort stands alone, which means you must "stack" your marketing efforts, building one on top of the other. For example, if you plan to advertise, perhaps place a banner or sign in front of your business to reflect the ad message, *plus* send out direct mail pieces to your customers to highlight the offer, *plus* sponsor a local event that will give your business even more exposure.

Marketing, by the way, knows no time frame. Remember I told you I didn't directly generate new business from my spot on CNNfn? I said *directly*. I plugged the event into my bio, used it in my pitches to clients, and displayed snippets of it on my website for years and years. This, coupled with my other marketing material, continues to lend credibility to my claims that I—and my business—can do a great job.

6. Find partners—lots of partners

By partners, I don't mean finding a business partner *per se*. Partners are everywhere—some share complementary services, others refer you because they know you're good. For example, Jen Rolston owns a small website design company, Eden Design. She runs a two-, sometimes three-person operation, and she's booked. She doesn't have the time or inclination to actually host the sites, but doesn't want to leave her clients hanging. So, she sends them to nearby Business Technology Source, which provides all the web support any business owner could want (cheerfully, by the way). This benefits everyone: Eden Design, which can provide a referral for its client; BTS, which gets more work;

and the client, who doesn't have to shop around for someone to host his site. And should BTS get a request for a website, it knows just where to send the customer. You'll hear more about BTS and co-owner Johnna Armstrong in chapter 8. Stay tuned!

7. Follow up, follow up, follow up

Yogi Berra once said, "It ain't over till it's over," and that's true no matter what impression your customers give you. Sure, they seemed interested, even enthusiastic, about your product or service. And sure, they agree that no one offers such a good deal. But still . . . they have to ask that ever-elusive spouse, CEO, or board of directors, depending on what you offer. So you wait . . . and wait . . . and hear nothing.

But before you think your marketing message has been in vain, follow up. That means shooting off an email reminding your customers that you're still around, asking them if they need more information, or suggesting another service or product they might enjoy. Going out of town for a week or two? Let them know and tell them when you'll return. If you own a retail operation, following up means maintaining exposure through free samples, notices that you're having a sale, new window displays, and other signals that you're alive and willing.

8. Collect every "no" to get "yes"

If you're anything like me, you want to be loved. You want your product, service, and marketing pitch to be loved, which means that you want to swim endlessly in a sea of "yes"—as unlikely, or even impractical, as that might be. But no one is loved by everyone. And not everyone is going to want your product, no matter how good your pitch or proposal. So try thinking of every "no" as a step toward "yes." Sometimes you can learn from them. For example, if a prospective client rejected your proposal because he found it confusing, better make a change. Other times, there's no lesson to learn. The prospect may have taken another course, hired his brother-in-law, gone bankrupt, or moved to the

Bahamas. Who knows? You sure don't. So stash that "no" for posterity, and keep searching for "yes."

9. Keep goals realistic

So, with all the wait and guesswork involved in marketing, how can you tell when your marketing is working? The signs will definitely be there, as long as your goals are reasonable and consistent with your industry. For example, if you're conducting cold calls, don't plan on getting a 50 percent "yes" rate. Generally, cold calls don't work that way. But 20 percent? That's something to brag about. And of that 20 percent, maybe two new clients? Not bad if each client brings in $50,000 contracts. And keep track: How many people responded to your ad campaign? How many saw your brochure? How many searched on the Web for your service or product and found you? Eventually, you can determine which marketing approach works best, although you should always keep your options—and your goals—open.

10. Try new things!

No marketing effort should ever be your last—no matter how well it works. So stay open. If your town is hosting an event, whether a folk concert or a political summit, look for marketing opportunities there. And keep your eyes open to the technology front. It seems that almost every day there are new ways to reach customers electronically.

Also, comb through the bookstore for new books on marketing-related matters. Join associations. Some, like the Direct Marketing Association (www.the-dma.org), tell you everything you need to know about marketing cold. Others, like the Society of Human Resource Management (www.shrm.org), can teach you everything you need to know about marketing to prospective employees—finding great people, an art in itself. And take risks. The more unique the greater the chance your message will be noticed and the better your business will do.

QUICK Tip

Ask Everyone: When I was first approached about writing this book, I thought, *Sure! A book on marketing? That's a snap.* I've been helping businesses manage their marketing forever. And I owned a small business that I had to market myself. How could there be any strategies I *didn't* know? But I decided to interview people anyway to find what worked best for them. Along the way, I discovered some cool new ideas, radical results, and interesting anecdotes. In fact, everyone I interviewed had another great idea to add to the list.

I've included these ideas here, and you should get some of your own, too. Just talk to successful business owners about what marketing ideas worked—and didn't work—for them. The businesses don't necessarily have to be in your line of work, either. And they don't have to be small. But I guarantee, everyone has at least one unique story to tell, and you'll benefit from each of them.

Marketing mavens

Should you hire someone to help with your marketing? Bring in a full-time person, perhaps? Naturally, the answer comes down to your marketing dollar and how difficult your marketing task. Thanks to the Web and marketing programs, many going as low as $20 for a complete and customized marketing set, you have plenty of choices. My advice is to market what you can. Hire a contractor to market what you can't. And have every employee—someway, somehow—market for you. Above all, keep control! You alone know the real value of your business, and no one can decide or publicize that for you.

Chapter 2

Marketing from Within: The Heart of Your Marketing Campaign

Ever been to a trade show? If so, you've noticed that after a few minutes, each booth, business, and product seem to blur into the next. Everyone has the same style of sign and giveaway—and whether it's pens, refrigerator magnets, or key chains, these promotional gifts tend to end up in the trash or between the cushions of your couch. Ask what they do, and you'll hear the same blurbs. Ask why they're different, and you'll hear the same comments that indicate how different they *aren't*. It seems everyone is "committed to meeting our customers' needs" and has "superior" products.

So why are their marketing approaches so similar—

especially since each business has its own unique characteristics, even when it offers the same products or services as another? The answer: business owners look to industry trends to determine their approaches. They follow rules. And they look for the right and wrong ways of doing things.

This isn't true of all businesses, of course. And the smart ones know about the concept of marketing from within. That's when you base your marketing campaign on the personality of your business—from your logo to the proposals you give to your customers. Essentially, in the words of pop psychologists everywhere, great marketing requires that businesses "be themselves." Stay true to your business, and your message will be unique and memorable.

By the way, marketing from within is the perfect antidote to spin. Why lie about your offering, stretch the truth, or give quality assurances that you just can't deliver? By marketing from within, you'll project the true benefits of your offering, and trust me, that will be good enough.

So how do you perfect the art of marketing from within? Tap into your business's true and unique marketing power? Start by reading through the questions in this chapter, and answer each question on Appendix A, Worksheet 1 (page 224). Take some time to think them through. Mull them over, even if the answer seems obvious. And use a pencil! You may want to change or add to your answer later.

Alert!

Contact the SBA: Marketing from within is different from marketing alone. You need feedback, support, and ideas! So, don't forget the Small Business Association. Sure, you'll meet prospective customers, but you'll also find it a bastion of great advice, feedback, and plenty of marketing smarts. Call your local SBA office, or get to it online at SBA.gov.

Ten Core Questions

1. What is your primary offering?

Okay, you're probably thinking that this is an outrageous first question. Of course you know your own product or service. That's why you run the business in the first place. But think again. You probably offer numerous services: at your office, at the client's site, or online. Or perhaps you offer unique or specialized products.

Regardless, you need to zero in on one particular offering. Sherry Squire, for example, owns a mediation service that helps businesses resolve employee-manager issues. She trains managers in communication techniques, develops manuals outlining crisis management steps, and conducts studies that help clients focus on the root of their problems.

But Sherry's core service is facilitating dialogue between managers, unions, and employees. Only when she focused on that specific function in everything from her tagline—Bringing Organizations Together Word by Word—to her brochures did the results from her marketing efforts start coming in. Naturally, once in the workplace, clients asked for her other services as well.

Now, answer Question 1 on Worksheet 1 (page 224). Don't be afraid to narrow down too much. You won't cancel out any of your valuable services; you'll just focus on the ones that matter most. If you're more comfortable creating a general category, fine, but don't make it *too* general. For example, if your business writes press releases, places articles for industry experts, and that sort of thing, you could say you provide public relations services. Still, narrow down a little in terms of your market. To corporations in crisis? To small, minority-owned businesses? Or maybe to financial institutions clamoring for exposure?

2. What is your secondary offering?

Your primary offering is anything that customers directly purchase. But in the business world, you're constantly marketing *everything*. Say you want to hire a new employee. The job market requires that you don't simply *announce* that position, but that you market it. Say you need to sell your employees on a new health plan. Marketing again. Other items are add-ons to your primary offering. Having a blow-out sale? Introducing a new product, employee, or office? You got it: marketing. It's important to consider everything you need to market as we move forward, for numerous reasons. The most critical: your marketing efforts need to be consistent to support and emphasize your most valuable commodity—your brand. Now, answer Question 2 on Worksheet 1.

3. Who is your customer?

The answer to this question might also seem obvious, but you'd be surprised. To start, you probably have a primary and secondary customer base to consider. The *primary* customers bring in the most business, are your best plug-in to customer networks, and are the ones you'll target in your marketing. Your *secondary* customers are the ones you get by default or circumstance. They're good, but not worth your marketing attention. For example, say you own a retail shop, like a shoe store. Your primary customers may be women in your community who frequent your shop. Your secondary customers may be tourists or other visitors who drop in on a whim, and vanish, leaving only a sales receipt behind.

If you're not sure about your primary customers, here's a quick Q&A. Already have a customer base? Read on anyway. You may need to redirect your marketing or narrow it further.

Q. How do I determine my customer base?

A. If you already have a business, look around and see who's there. Are you happy with that customer base? Or do your customers simply interfere with your ability to reach your financial goals? If so, who would be a better customer? Try to base your responses on concrete information, such as the income level of your customers, the number of competitors in your market, and any new opportunities that might be springing up.

Q. Once I've established a customer base, should I stick with it or change?

A. Stagnation is the enemy of any business owner. If you see an opportunity, go for it. But beware of false leads or the possibility that you'll spread yourself too thin. And remember, never leave a customer behind. If you have a new direct mail campaign or a special offer targeting a new customer group, for example, include the old ones, too.

Q. Should I have separate campaigns for my primary and secondary customers?

A. Possibly. But remember, marketing takes time, money, and plenty of energy. Use these wisely.

Now, answer the next set of questions on Worksheet 1. We'll consolidate this information at the end of this section to help you develop a great marketing plan.

4. Who are your major competitors?

Your major competitors may come in three forms:

Immediate competitors. If you have a small retail operation, you can probably see them across the street or around the block. If you offer services, perhaps you saw their ads or heard about them from colleagues. Or maybe you own a franchise. If so, the parent company may have tipped you off to specific competitors and their exact locations.

Distant competitors. You can't see them, but every moment, you know they're there. If you happen to own a small hardware store, for example, you're competing with other small hardware stores, but also those big warehouse operations like Lowe's and Home Depot that may be miles away. If you're a consultant, you may be competing against the big guys like KPMG and Coopers & Lybrand. Regardless, identify them.

Virtual competitors. Just about everything you can buy in person, you can get online. That goes for medical advice, precious gems, even husbands. Your competitors may lurk somewhere in cyberland—so don't forget about them!

5. What distinguishes you from your competitors?

A few points regarding this very important question:

To start, when considering your competitors, you may be tempted to use words like pathetic, unprofessional, and rip-off artists. In fact, most people treat competitors like menaces to the profession and far, far beneath their considerably higher standards. Try to avoid this thinking. It doesn't help. It only makes you resentful.

A second matter goes back to the marketing from within idea. Before you look out at your competitors and decide, "Hmm, here's how I'm going to be different," decide what qualities best speak to your business culture. Are you exceptionally skilled? Do you offer a wide range of services in a field that hardly offers a grain of salt? Perhaps you have a specialty, or maybe it's you personally. Do people love you? Your answer will be central to your marketing approach.

CASE STUDY: DISTINGUISH YOUR BUSINESS

Two shoe stores, Larsen's and Marcus Shoes, occupy the same street. Both carry women's shoes, although they have an impressive selection for men. Both are small. And both cater to the same customers, more or less. But that's where the similarities end.

Marcus Shoes is orderly, shoes placed just so on the rack. Want to know if they have your size? No scrounging through shelves hidden somewhere out back. No pulling open boxes for a missing pair. No, these guys have everything cataloged in a computer so they can find the precise location of your shoe in seconds. The employees rotate, so you're never quite sure whom you'll get, but guaranteed, he'll be professional. As for the owner, he's a slick, well-dressed man who walks the short path to fashion, and will gladly show you around, footwear first.

Larsen's is . . . well, if you have kids, imagine their bedroom at its worst: toys and boxes strewn around the floor; clothes draped over a chair, flung over a dresser. Now, add lots and lots of shoes, shoeboxes, and very little room to move. This, I must tell you, is Larsen's.

So, you may think that Marcus's has the competitive upper hand, right? Not so. Larsen's has a true competitive difference. They don't push it or exploit it—but they live it, and signal it on the front door: "The Friendly Shoe Store"—and that's no line.

The store is owned by a father-daughter team. Walk through the door and they not only greet you, but remember a conversation you had weeks—even months—before. The prices aren't listed in their computer—there is no computer. Plan to spend extra time as they hunt for your size or one reasonably close, chatting and joking as they do.

Larsen's or Marcus's? Most people pick both.

6. How much does your business rely on *you*?

Small-business owners usually play an enormous role in whether people choose their offerings. Think about the small businesses you frequent, especially the three- or four-person operations. You probably know the owner, and probably go there partially for them. Now, think about your local Starbucks or McDonald's. Who owns that?

Granted, sometimes your employees or a partner might be the front person for your operation. Say you offer a service like hosting websites or processing data. Your customers' primary human contact is with a salesperson or employee who troubleshoots problems. That doesn't mean you're off the hook. You still establish the organizational culture that's reflected in your marketing approach.

7. Do you have any special talents that could give you a marketing edge?

Obviously, I don't mean talents like juggling—especially if you're, say, a doctor. But you may be a great writer. If so, consider writing opinion pieces that give your expertise exposure. Perhaps you're great with people: quick with a joke, great with a handshake. Definitely show up at as many local fairs, trade shows, or other events as appropriate and possible. Or maybe the motto "I never met a mic I didn't like" applies to you, and you let loose anytime a podium is available or television camera turns your way. Feature this talent by hosting local events, running TV ads, or speaking at professional conferences.

8. What do you think? A quick list of adjectives

Turn to Worksheet 1 (Question 8, of course) and write ten adjectives that best reflect you, your business, even your primary product. Adjectives, in case you don't remember from high school, are those words that describe nouns. Like "savory," "sumptuous," and "delectable," which might work if you own a restaurant. But don't try these if you're a researcher at a hospital.

Only a few rules before you proceed:

• No modesty. Save modesty for a blind date. This requires candor and ego.

• No qualifiers. Resist touting the middle line by saying things like "relatively bright" or "pretty interesting." You're "brilliant" and "provocative."

• No mulling. Just write.

• By the way, if you don't own the business because someone else does, you have a partner, or you're heading up a nonprofit, don't worry. You can still participate by describing the product, service, or general culture at work.

Now, go through your list and circle the four or five adjectives that are the most dissimilar. For example, if you said: "savory," "sumptuous," "delectable," "healthy," "nutritious," and "inexpensive," you'd cut "sumptuous" and "nutritious," because they are basically the same as "delectable" and "healthy." You should use the remaining words at some point in your brochures, website, even on your business cards, perhaps with a tagline that reads: "Where delectable meets healthy at a reasonable price," or something like it. If all the words add something new, cut the ones that are lowest on your priority list.

9. What do your customers think? Another quick list of adjectives

Maybe you know how customers describe you or your business, so yes, you can list the adjectives now. But soon, confirm what you know. Trust me, you'll definitely be surprised. Take Sherry (she owned that mediation business we discussed earlier). She assumed customers considered her "quick," "lively," "available," "friendly," and "responsive." Then she questioned her customers. They agreed to all these descriptors but, lo and behold, felt one was even more fitting: intelligent. In fact, *every* client came up with "intelligent" or a word close to it. She embedded that in her marketing copy soon after.

Getting this information is easy. Here are some common ways:

• *Email queries.* Email your favorite clients and ask them to list ten adjectives that best describe you. Don't provide detail or limit what they say. Just ask for the first examples that come to their minds. Whatever you do, don't have a subject line saying "Customer Survey." They'll expect some long, drawn-out questionnaire and will delete your email faster than spam. Instead, try using something like "A Quick Question." No fuss, no bother. They open, list, and they're done.

Remember, in essence this is asking your customers to work for you, so you can also offer something business-related in return. But make it easy on yourself, too—no hour-long consulting sessions, free products, or anything that might cause your profit margins to drop.

• *Phone calls.* These can be helpful, too, since they give you the opportunity to ask questions about their answer. For example, if a client told Sherry he thought her services were "intelligent," she'd have the opportunity to say, "Interesting; how so?" Then, he'd provide details that Sherry could use now in her marketing materials and, quite possibly, to help her make decisions about what services to add or drop. Whether you, an employee, or a professional service should make these calls depends on your relationship with the customer. But make sure you (or someone else high up in the company) contact VPs, business owners, and others higher up the chain. As with the emails, keep the discussion short.

• *Focus groups.* Focus groups are more time-consuming and expensive, depending on whether you outsource the meetings or conduct them yourself. Basically, you get a group of customers or target customers into a room and ask questions. Maybe you want feedback about your goods and services. Maybe you want to know what they like best about your packaging. Let the dialogue flow. And take notes. Lots of them.

By the way, if you already have this information, get it again at some point. Your clients' perceptions will change as your business and offerings grow.

10. What do your customers want?

So, what do your customers really want? This question is different from the previous one. Whatever their impression of your brand or identity, they may desire a totally unrelated primary product or service. Tapping into the changing pulse of their needs may prove critical to the continued success of your business. Just think about all the successful businesses you know that folded. One reason: the owners didn't vary their offerings as time required. Or, just as likely, they didn't engage in sufficient marketing to let their customers know the offerings changed.

Yes, you can address this question on Worksheet 1 now. But keep a regular tally anyway, now and for the life of your business. If you own a nonprofit, keep an eye on related issues that concern your benefactors most. If you're marketing a job, be alert to changes in the job market and your specific industry.

All the methods we covered in Question 9—emails, phone calls, and focus groups—can help address this question. But let's add three more to your list:

• *Suggestion and comment boxes.* Keep these handy cards, with a nicely designed box, in some convenient location. Beware of the box gravitating to a dusty corner or getting chipped, shriveled, or dilapidated.

The suggestion box is its own marketing tool, telling customers you care about them. It takes the "tailored to your needs" cliché to real-life levels.

• *Research*. This probably sounds more intense than it is—the world is already filled with interesting statistics broken into countless demographics. You already described your primary customer. So, in your research, track down everything you can find about that group. The Web is your best friend here, although if you belong to an association or read industry magazines, you'll pick up plenty of cues.

• *Look and listen*. Keep an eye out for newspaper articles, trade magazine features, and other sources that will tip you off to customer trends. Be prepared to provide your products online. Maybe offer DVDs. Providing consulting services? A new line of requirements will be sprouting up (and vanishing) just about every day. Think about knowledge management. Whatever happened to *that*?

CASE STUDY: RESPOND TO YOUR MARKET

On the local front, you may not have to open your ears and eyes—they may be opened for you. Take Rusty Berry. He bought an old turn-of-the-century theater called the Opera House. Since operas rarely came to town—okay, *never* came to town—and since his customer base didn't like operas anyway, he decided to show movies instead. He revamped the theater, added a screen, and voilà. Build it and they will come. Right?

But Rusty had bigger ideas. He wanted to return the theater to the days of old with a twist: host concerts, folk festivals, and other live entertainment. So he took down the movie screen, arranged some concerts, and reopened the doors. But not too many people came. Sure, he could have publicized his offerings more frequently, tried new marketing approaches, tapped into new potential markets . . . except for one problem.

Rusty and his wife, Pam, were practically assaulted by local residents demanding the movies. The market, dry cleaners, nowhere was safe.

> People claimed their weekends were ruined. Their social options dimmed. They practically turned the Opera House movies into a civic duty. So Rusty kept the movie reels rolling with live shows in between.
>
> Build it? Sure. But look, listen, respond, and market, *then* they will come.

Congratulations!

You have just laid the groundwork that will shape your marketing efforts and drive your business forward. Now, go back to Worksheet 1 and review your answers. Do they seem on target? Do you want to reconsider your customer? Your competition? Then, move on to chapter 3. Keep the pencil out and get ready to perfect one of the most important aspects of your marketing effort.

Chapter

3

Love You,
Love Your Brand

Your brand is what sets your company apart from the others: it's your image, your distinguishing feature, what people identify with when they think of you. It makes your business distinct. Visible. And it drives people to you. Not *all* people—no one is liked by everyone—but the *right* people, the primary customers who respond best to your offerings. You've already defined your business and laid the groundwork for projecting your brand to the world, so roll up your proverbial sleeves and get ready! The development phase has begun!

QUICK Tip

Bringing in Experts: You might wonder whether you should formulate your brand by yourself or hire a specialist to help you. Plenty of PR firms, marketing specialists, image consultants, and just about every other kind of consultant imaginable can help. But consider a few points before you decide to farm out or do the work yourself:

• You must have the final say over your brand. No one knows your business as well as you, and ultimately, no one else can make these kinds of critical decisions.

• Think budget! Marketing can suck you in like a black hole—that leaves you in the red. Every step of the way, you'll have the option to hire a specialist.

• Think timing, too! If you do hire experts, try bringing them in as a checkup for the tail end of the process, when possible. Or bring them in at the beginning to help you carve the way. In a sense, they'll function like consultants, giving you feedback and advice, without doing the work.

• Determine your strengths and weaknesses, and above all, trust your gut! You'll know when you need some help—but don't underestimate your own abilities.

Three Keys to Establishing Your Brand

Establishing your brand takes three key ingredients. They're important and can make the difference between a powerful presence in your field and a dull message no one notices, let alone remembers. Read these carefully, and keep them in mind as you develop, shape, and even change your marketing approach.

1. Authenticity

Try not to develop a brand based solely on the market or one that goes against the grain of your competitors' efforts. You'll only end up sounding like everyone else. Worse, though, is if you succeed and attract customers hoping for one thing and getting another. I'm sure you've experienced this at one time or another with companies promising to be friendly or to provide great customer service, then treating you as an unwelcome guest at a funeral.

Instead, focus on what's really there, using the marketing from within approach we talked about in the previous chapter. Will your marketing approach rely on your personality and your presence? If so, what is your personality? What do people like about you, especially in the business sense? If it's your product, what makes it better? Unique? Focus on these matters, looking at what's *really* there.

2. Consistency

Once you determine your brand, consistency is key. Every aspect—and I mean *every* aspect—should reflect that brand, including:
- Company and product names
- Your website
- Clothes your employees wear at work and at the client site
- The design of your lobby, building, or shop
- Marketing materials: brochures, tip sheets, white papers, and emails
- Your employees' approach to the customer
- Hours of operation

For example, if you want your business to have a friendly, laid-back feel, make sure your office has comfortable chairs; a ready-and-waiting coffee pot and tea kettle; appropriate hours; accessible marketing materials and tip sheets; calm, friendly employees; and relaxed colors—not, for example, neon oranges and greens, bright reds, or dull-as-dust grays. We'll talk more about perfecting these elements of your brand later.

3. Follow-through

People are great at defining a brand. Their creative juices get flowing, their brain starts chugging, and ideas flow faster than water in a flood. And they come up with some really snazzy ads, logos, and even home pages for their websites.

Then, the whole thing stops. Every new product, service, employee, brochure . . . every new everything follows the same old format using the same old words as everyone else—as if that brand didn't exist. The marketing material becomes boring. *Really* boring. In fact, it's so boring, you can't tell one from another, which is okay, because trust me, no one notices anyway.

So, be sure that every change you make to your business somehow reflects your brand. Want to change direction? Want to tweak or revamp because, somehow, that brand just isn't you or your organization anymore? Go ahead. Just remember points one and two of this list when you do.

QUICK Tip

Brand Consistency: To get a big-business example for small-business branding, think about two companies. One is Southwest Airlines: friendly, casually dressed employees; reasonable rates; and humorous announcements as the plane takes off—especially useful for those suffering from a fear of flying. The other is Nike. The shoes, with the omnipresent logo; the website that has so much energy your computer might implode; and the language so cool, so driven, you think even the letters work out. Consistent. Effective. Great.

So what are the lessons for you, especially if you don't have a gazillion-dollar advertising budget? Simply apply this:

Brand + Marketing + Consistency = Customers

Repeat as needed.

Name That Brand: Three Rules for Making Your Name

Remember that Shakespearean saying from Romeo and Juliet: "What's in a name? That which we call a rose / By any other name would smell as sweet"? Well, no offense to The Great Writer, but what's in a name is an entire marketing campaign. It tells people particulars about your offering. It helps them remember that you're there in the first place. It gives them something to identify with. And it establishes expectations that you'll undoubtedly meet. All this in a millisecond. Yes, names are the essence of instant marketing, and finding the right name is less expensive than almost free. It costs you nothing.

Sooner or later, you'll need to concoct names. Lots of them—for products, special events, newsletters, and sales. Depending on what you do, the list can be endless. And then, of course, there's the name of your organization. If you're in business, names are just a part of life. And here's what you *must* remember:

1. Make it sayable

Don't you love those business owners who insist on using their own names for their business? You end up with "Rackanicov, Bamberdeanian & Sons." This is a surefire network-opportunity stopper: who will pass your name on when no one can say it? Also, beware of those embarrassing names where you mean to say one thing but end up saying something altogether different. I once had a friend who worked for a small gourmet restaurant called "Pini's Pantry." Pini, by itself, sounds fine, but add that "s" and say it fast enough . . . needless to say, the employees were too embarrassed to answer the phone.

2. Make it informative

Make sure the name tells the prospective customer something about the business. The more specific the better. A company like "Business Solutions" could be promising anything from office supplies to temporary help. But the "Sweet Shoppe Bakery" states it pretty clearly, and visions of Danishes, cookies, and mile-high cupcakes (the frosting vaguely reminiscent of a bouffant hairdo) practically drift before your eyes. The following are good examples, too:

• *The Coffee and Candlery.* The name focuses on the store's two central products, although it provides a lot more, with a fun twist that reflects the owner and the overall atmosphere when you walk in.

• *Step On Out.* A high-fashion shoe store whose offerings make you want to get dancing.

• *Goose Route Dance Company.* Okay, the goose part may not be entirely obvious, but the company is located on the Potomac and Shenandoah Rivers, where geese frequently fly overhead.

• *Winchester Oil Company.* Based in Winchester, Virginia, it provides home heating oil. Need they say more?

• *Elegance Home Fineries.* Most definitely *not* a consignment shop.

Aside from pronunciation problems, you can get into trouble if you use your name for your business, since it doesn't reveal anything about your offering. Of course, if you boast high name recognition, like, say, "The Tom Cruise Acting School," or "Bill Clinton Center for International Relations," go ahead. Ditto if you want your brand to revolve entirely around you.

3. Make sure name = brand

If you're trying to reflect a fun, upbeat company, then you certainly don't want to name it Grayson & Sons, LLC. But if you have a D.C. lobbying firm, Fun Among Us (the name of a toy store in Gloucester, Massachusetts) most certainly wouldn't do the trick, revealing as it may be.

Remember, every time you stamp a product, service, sale, or anything else with a name, it must reflect your business and your brand. Fun Among Us, for example, wouldn't feature a section called Pedagogical Play Instruments for Toddlers. That might be fine if you hosted a toy sale in an educational research institute . . . but maybe not. More likely they'd use something like Teaching Toys for Tots.

So what happens if you have an up-and-running business but the name doesn't reflect your brand? Or the name is simply boring, but you've had it so long, you don't dare change it? Here are a few possibilities:

• *Follow the Kentucky Fried lead.* Here's an example of a company whose market shifted from family eating to teenage hip. But consumers *still* identified Kentucky Fried Chicken with the old image. Rather than drop the name altogether—an impossibility given factors like customer recognition—they repositioned it and it became KFC.

• *Change the tagline.* Once you have a name, you're more or less stuck with it. But the tagline? That's a different story. Taglines come and go like gift wrap, depending on whom you're trying to market to and when. We'll talk about taglines later, but for now, suffice it to say, consider your name a marriage but your tagline a date.

• *Shift the image.* The visuals—whether on your logo, letterhead, business card, or just about anywhere else—will speak worlds about the name. Have a gray background, but trying to reach a fast-paced, urban consumer? Think bold yellows and greens. Trying to attract kids? How about adding paisleys or balloon-like circles among the stripes?

Web smarts

Want people to go online to order your product? Want them to visit your shop? What better way to market than to build the address into your name? Think, for example, of one of the Web's leading shopping malls, especially known for its books. You're thinking, no doubt, about Amazon.com. And here is the question *no one* will ever ask: "What is their web address exactly?" So why not give your service, business, or product a dot-com name? Your customer will know where to go when they need you.

As for street addresses, the same principle works. Only in the virtual world, you make your address and home into whatever image you please. If your real-life address is in the shady part of town, better not use it, unless, of course, you want customers who appreciate those settings.

Another consideration is the name of the street. If you happen to house your business at, say, 77 Shrub Hill, maybe not—unless you own a nursery. But 77 Lansdowne Street? Sounds great, doesn't it?

Finally, street addresses work well if they happen to speak about your enterprise. We mentioned Shrub Hill. But how about if you happen to design clothing on Fashion Boulevard? The name will work whether you use it for the business, a line of clothing, your newsletter, or even a tagline, as in "Betsy Martin Design: Where Fashion begins on Fashion Boulevard."

> ### QUICK Tip
>
> Idea Shopping: To get your creative-name juices flowing, be alert. You can get all sorts of ideas from other companies. The next time you're driving down a street cluttered with stores, for example, look at the names in front. Or examine the labels of your clothes. You'll find some surprising creativity there. Check the packages you purchase. Starbucks must have hundreds of names for everything from their seasonal offerings to their ordinary blends. If you're looking at ads in a magazine or newspaper, see if you can find interesting names for particular events or sales. And definitely surf the Web, especially for businesses like yours. Find examples you don't like? Take note! Be aware of what you don't like about them and avoid those mistakes yourself.
>
> Now, go to Worksheet 2. You'll find some questions there related to names—not only for your business, but also for specific offerings.

AAA (All About Acronyms)

These days, it seems the world loves an acronym. From the restaurant chain TGIF to government agencies like the IRS, acronyms reign. But will acronyms help or hinder your marketing effort? That depends on how you use them. Here are some tips for acronyms. They apply not only to your name, but to the text in your marketing material as well.

• Only use acronyms your reader can say and hear in their inner ear when they see it in print. Plenty of names sound like XRT-12. Sounds like a prescription drug you definitely wouldn't want to take. That's not a door-opener for marketing.

• Make sure your acronym directly connects with your offering. TGIF, while cumbersome to say, does connect with the words all of us feel at least one day a week: Thank God It's Friday.

• Don't let acronyms that only other industry professionals understand creep into your marketing literature. Your reports, okay. Even your proposals. But you never know who's going to glance through that brochure, tip sheet, or web page, and the decision-maker may know nothing about the mechanics of your offering, only that he needs the end result it promises.

• Define the acronym if you must, but don't use the traditional form of writing out the name and putting the acronym in parenthesis, as in Thank God It's Friday (TGIF). Marketing must have pizzazz, which means keeping as far from the routine, boring, or menacingly conventional as possible. Instead, reveal the full name creatively, either through some interesting graphic device, in your return address, or in your tagline.

TGIF now calls itself "TGI Friday's"—emphasis on the "Friday." And their tagline is undeniable: "Everyone could use more Fridays."

Taglines

We've mentioned taglines already, but let's look at them more closely. Everyone loves a great tagline. And because you have more words to work with than your name alone, you can let loose. It only takes one good tag, and your customers are instantly hooked. The brand is there, emblazoned in their minds, leading them to the product. Just take this quick quiz and identify whose taglines appear below:

• Just do it
• Be all that you can be
• Mmmm, mmmm, good
• When it rains, it pours

You'd be a rare exception if you didn't know the Nike tagline. And the army competed with the best of them with the corporate "Be all that you can be" logo years ago. Campbell's Soup's "Mmmm, mmmm, good" is a classic, especially with a little Morton's salt that pours when it rains and, I assume, when it doesn't. When your tagline is good, you create an image that stays with your customer.

How do you create a tagline? It's one part creativity, one part science, and one part trial, test, and trial again. Here's what I mean:

- **Creativity**. Unlike just about every other aspect of your business, from picking a health plan to managing cash flow, marketing cannot be boiled down to a formula. So let go, have a little fun. Play with all the possibilities. One clothing store featuring feathery boas, lacy gloves, and other offbeat garments has this tagline: "Fluff with substance." Great, isn't it?
- **Science**. No matter what, make sure your tagline has these qualities:
  - Quick and easy to say. Don't go beyond six words; three is ideal. Little words like "the" and "and" don't count.
  - Reflects your brand. "Fluff with substance" is great for an offbeat clothing store catering to the more creative instinct within us, but a definite nonstarter for, say, a dating service.
  - Rolls off the tongue—and straight into your customer's memory.
  - Provides information. The tagline "When it rains, it pours," alludes to the clumpy form other salt brands take in humidity. Not the most compelling reason to buy the salt, but what else is there? The taste?

Take a cue from those adjectives you and your primary customers used to describe your business. If one of them is "professional," allude to the professional nature of your business in your tag. If "humor" cropped up, all the better. Make your tagline fun!

- **Trial, test, and trial again**. Show your tagline. Not to everyone—remember, when marketing, you're never trying to reach the world. You *are* trying to reach your primary customers. They're the ones who count.

You can get this feedback formally through focus groups, although that probably isn't necessary. Instead, just ask. Ask which sample people like the most. Or have them read three samples, and a few minutes later, ask which one they remember.

If you're stuck for ideas, here are some strategies to get you through. Businesses everywhere use them, so they'll probably sound familiar.

Tagline: Belonging

Never underestimate our instinct to be part of the crowd. And you can get your customers to feel like they belong in only a few quick words—all of

them common but amazingly effective:
- The #1 brand
- The leading brand
- Billions and billions (or however many) served
- Most popular in Denver (or anywhere else)

In case you think this language is reserved for the lowest common denominator, forget it. The *New York Times* book section contains ads touting a book as "The #1 Bestseller." Even better, these taglines are sound-bite testimonials: "#1 Bestseller" rolls thousands of accolades into two little words. CompUSA has this tagline: "Where America Buys Technology." Who could argue with that?

Tagline: Nostalgia

It is nostalgia and only nostalgia that compels us to purchase products that make the following claims:
- Roofers (or whatever) since 1938
- Providing specialty service for over 60 years
- Your friends in the business since 1952
- The oldest bookstore (or whatever) in New England
- The Original!

In this age of the mega-corporation, longevity really means something. The little guys are swallowed up by the big ones; the old traditional stores have a new, corporate soul. Besides, we have historical, sentimental attachment to products—if it was good enough for my mother, grand-mother, and great-grandmother, why, it's good enough for me!

Tagline: Sentiment

Be careful of this one. When it works it works, when it doesn't: instant sap! Still, plenty of advertisers use the sentimental tag successfully, depending on their offering. If you happen to manufacture drill bits, the sentimental approach probably won't work. But anything personal, from food to clothing, resounds with possibility.

Here are a few examples:
- The way a home ought to be (housing development)
- Teach your child the 3 R's (a tutoring service)
- Just like your mother use to make (restaurant)

Tagline: Exclusivity

What is the difference between an old pine cupboard and a new one? The answer: there are more new pine cupboards around. And that, in a nutshell, is how antiques have gained their value in the world. Only an exclusive few have them. But antiques aren't the only such items. You can build exclusivity into your brand with tags like these:
- For the discriminating buyer
- The outstanding collection for outstanding people
- Special edition
- Not like everyone else

The exclusivity line, by the way, is a *must* for any sale, opening, or introduction to a new line of product, a new senior partner, and so on.

CASE STUDY: AND THE TAGLINE PRIZE GOES TO . . .

Granted, this isn't a small business. But the tagline is great—100 percent pure technology; fast, immediate, very futuristic. If you're thinking IBM or Microsoft, guess again. I'm referring to True Temper golf clubs. That's right, golf clubs. Actually, the golf club *shafts*. Here's what they say, with a hint of "belonging" thrown in:

The #1 Shaft in Golf:

"Frequency Tuned . . . Grip to Tip Tapered Technology"

By the way, note the name of the shaft: Black Gold. It could be Pink Green or Violet Amber. Or how about Paste Hued? These are colors we're talking about and one is as good, performance-wise, as another. But Black Gold is all about brand.

QUICK Tip

Use the Whole Team: Having trouble conjuring a tagline? Are you better at crunching numbers or compiling reports than writing quick and pithy one-liners? Then try this strategy for pulling together a great tagline. It will cost you time, but that's it. Get together everyone on your team: your employees, part-time support staff, even subcontractors if you're a one- or two-person operation. Discuss your primary offering, your competitors, your primary customer, and the other points we discussed in the previous chapter. Make sure they have a general "feel" for your brand—be it funny, technologically astute, highbrow, or hip.

Then have everyone write at least ten ideas for a tagline—don't worry about word count. Have them write fast—no stopping or editing. If your team is short on meeting time, have them write their ideas beforehand and bring them to the meeting. Read the tags aloud without mentioning any names. Knock off the ones that don't fit and save the rest. Then cross out the weaker options and keep the strongest.

Then pick one or two you like best and tweak, tweak, and tweak some more until you have a tagline that works. If you're really motivated, ask customers, friends, even strangers for their feedback. Stay as close to your primary customer as possible; if you sell skateboards, don't ask a mother with five young kids or an elderly resident at a nursing home.

Now, go to Worksheet 2 and complete the tagline portion. Remember, this is *not* an exercise. Use real taglines for your real service or product. Be sure to get feedback when you're done.

A Picture Says a Thousand (Marketing) Words

Images are the epitome of instant marketing. Customers see them, whether they want to or not, whether they know it or not. With words, they must choose to read. But images just flow right in. Perhaps the most valuable—and underrated—aspect of images as marketing tools is the power of association. With just the right image, your customer will associate your business with whatever feeling, memory, or concept you desire.

Take the Morton salt girl. The yellow slicker and bright umbrella conjure all sorts of home, hearth, and old-fashioned goodness associations. As for Harley Davidson, their legendary black with a touch of fire orange conjures associations of danger, renegade exploration, and the twenty-first-century cowboy. Hey, as their tagline says, "It's a big world. Saddle up and ride." The prim and prissy are not invited.

Alert!

Pictures, Pictures Everywhere: You need images in every marketing piece you create, whether it's a logo on your stationery or photos on your website. They break the black-and-white of words and suggest something more fun, serious, professional, or intense is at hand. Besides, people need a reason to read even a word (yes, a word!) of marketing material, so your image may lure them in, or be the *only* message they receive. You can identify the picture of the Morton Salt girl. But do you know what the writing on the salt container says?

Here are some homes for your images:
- Website
- Brochures
- Business cards
- Newsletter
- Holiday greeting cards
- Proposals
- Invitations
- Ads
- Posters
- Calendars and other gift items
- Window displays
- Signs
- Press kit
- Packaging
- Bags and other containers
- Lobby
- Showroom

Imagery Dos and Don'ts

Do: Use fresh images your customer will enjoy. If you happen to own a CPA practice in a mountainous retreat, go ahead and put a design, or even a photo, of a mountain in your material.

Don't: Use pictures that reek of sentimentalism, when the sentimental value is entirely yours. A classic example: small-business brochures with a picture of the owner and her family, pets and all. A good reason to shop there? Don't think so. An attractive, even remotely interesting photo? Usually not. But if you *must*, save it for the holidays. Ditto for photos of the office clan.

Do: Use consistent images. If you're going with the cheetah, stay with the cheetah or other wild-animal theme.

Don't: Stray into cute. Sure, you may run a pediatrics clinic or a veterinary hospital. But keep it tasteful. No one wants to go to a professional whom they associate with a Hallmark card.

Do: Be sure the image fits with your overall brand. You *can* be indirect, of course. If you own that CPA firm I mentioned earlier, you're staying consistent with your brand by showing a mountainscape and not, say, a spreadsheet with numbers. Your brand is the *feeling* of what you do, not the task or product you offer.

Don't: Use an image just because you like it. It's an essential part of your marketing package—make sure it fits.

Do: Use images with a promise of movement and energy. You can suggest movement through the blurriness of a camera shot or even the aftermath of an event—people crowding around the winner of a sporting event, with the tagline "We get you there . . ." beneath it.

Don't: Please, of all things, do not have loads of pictures of people sitting around a table, looking at some inscrutable piece of paper and smiling. Or staring into a computer, hard at work. Or any other stagnant image where the people could be developing the newest form of software or writing spam. These types of images are totally generic and say nothing about the unique, compelling nature of your company.

Finding Visuals

By visuals, we mean everything from your logo to photos for your website to package design to the look of your brochures. The list is endless. And important—the right visual gets an instant response. The wrong visual, and you're forever forgotten. Visuals support your tagline, your name, and all your marketing efforts. They function much like the soundtrack to a thriller movie. Turn down the volume, and the effect is gone.

Basically, you can take three directions to find the perfect visual to match your brand.

1. Do it yourself

These days, with the number of computer marketing programs around, the do-it-yourself option is a breeze. Software companies offer such vast quantities of clip art that reflecting your individual brand with mass-marketed templates and designs is not a bad option.

In fact, Nova puts out a business card software package that promises you thirty-five thousand clip art images and, as they say in their tagline, "millions of unique possibilities." This may seem like a lot until you see the My Software package, which promises a million photos and images. How many possibilities is that?

Even better, there's a software package for just about every type of marketing material you want to create, with templates that make producing material a matter of cutting and pasting. The pricing is pretty reasonable, ranging from about $9.99 to $49.99. Publisher Pro, by the way, offers what their tagline deems the "fastest, easiest way to create documents with impact," including web pages, greeting cards, and ads, for $89.99. (By the way, their package might be a steal but their tagline could use some help!)

Even Hallmark, the card maker who put the "sap" in "sappy," has greeting card software complete with seven thousand cards and projects, twelve thousand clip art images (complete with puppies and kittens, I assume), and an unidentified quantity of "Exclusive Hallmark fonts." If you happen to be in drilling or septic tanks, Hallmark may not be the best for you. But if you own a pet supply store, crafts store, or other such enterprise, Hallmark may be the way to go for holiday greeting cards.

Perhaps the best news is that the programs allow you to print on demand. If you're visiting a client or attending a meeting, you can print out exactly what you need and not waste money producing hundreds more.

Having said that, the do-it-yourself option is loaded with hidden costs. Perhaps the most expensive is your or your employees' time. Unless you're a graphic designer, you probably have a learning curve that could take up potentially billable hours or unnecessary quantities of your valuable energy. Then there's the cost of color ink, hovering around $49.99 a refill, and the cost of paper. The price here ranges: Avery offers one hundred sheets for trifold brochures at $19.99 while fifty sheets of HP Advent brochure and flyer paper cost about $24.99.

Either way, weigh the pros and cons before deciding whether to go it alone. The only thing about software that's certain these days is every price ends with a ".99."

2. Have someone do it for you

The cost of this can be a bit startling at first, especially if you don't have piles of money in your budget. The average cost of a business card with logo can be thousands of dollars; ditto for your basic brochure. That's *without* copies. The hidden costs can add up, too, including time. When I hired a web designer to build my site, she was late by weeks with every draft for my approval. Then, a few impatient months down the pike—and my site still not live—she informed me she was exhausted and going away for three weeks. When my website finally did appear in cyberworld, I was thrilled, albeit worn-out from the experience.

Remember, even the promptest professionals have other clients besides you; monogamy just isn't the rule. That means you must wait days, weeks, or sometimes even longer while they bestow their attention on someone else. Even the big guys, like OfficeMax, make you wait two weeks to copy business cards. If time really is money, you might go broke waiting.

The good news, of course, is that they, not you, do the work. Aside from helping you focus on your area of expertise, this arrangement promises you'll have a professional applying hers. In spite of the time I waited for my website and logo to come through, I was pretty happy with the results. And making a few changes required nothing more than a quick email to the designer.

3. Both

This is perhaps the best option. You do your part and they do theirs. For example, you may want to design your own brochure but have a professional customize your logo. And since most of the packages let you import graphics, you can easily cut and paste it in. Or you may want to develop everything—from your letterhead to giveaway calendars—at your own desktop, but have someone else do the printing. This is especially useful if you attend lots of conferences and need thousands of brochures. The cost is almost negligible and the benefit of having someone deliver pre-folded, ready-to-go copies is obvious. Just make sure you have room to store them.

QUICK Tip

Appeal to Their Fantasy: Let's say you own a furniture store and want to display your offerings in a photo. Do you show it in a fancy, upscale house or a comfy suburban home? The answer depends on your primary customers: who they are, how they see themselves, and who they want to be! Highly successful professionals at mid-management levels? Adventurous types who spend their weekends mowing the lawn? Upscale entrepreneurs with middle-class incomes? Car ads are a perfect example of this. Who actually drives a new car up a steep mountain cliff or through a desert? Not many people—but plenty of suburbanites looking for a new car to comfortably fit the dog, kids, and the stroller wish they could.

How About Those Logos?

If you want to create a logo yourself, go for it. You'll create one like no one else has—and the almost-free cost (consider your time an expense) is fabulous. Of course, you can design your logo solo and get help later. For example, I have a friend who conducts lyric-writing classes to groups nationwide and boosts a bevy of famous friends. He needed a logo that was spiffy, sharp, and professional on an unspiffy budget. So, he designed his own logo.

Amazingly, he did a great job. I say "amazingly" because the guy had *no* graphic design experience, or talent, as far as I knew. When round two of copying and tweaking the material rolled around, though, he hired a professional to fine-tune. The result was slicker and better, but not profoundly so. And the price was pennies compared to the hundreds—even thousands—of dollars he would have spent had he hired a pro to do the job from Day One.

Whether or not you create your own logo, take the following steps. They apply to packaging, signs, and other visual components of your marketing effort.

1. Comb the Web

Look for as many logo ideas as you can muster. Consider the elements of your brand—do you see yourself as energetic? Jazzy? Get online and look for other companies who share these qualities. They don't necessarily have to share your product or service, although checking the competitors' logos can give you perspective.

2. Determine the design

Basically, you can choose from three different styles of logos:

• A logo that illustrates what you do. For example, if you own a café, you'd probably have an image of a coffee grinder or a steaming cup of coffee in the background. Make airplane parts? You'd probably show an airplane of some sort.

• A logo that centers on a graphic. These don't have to connect directly to your product or service. For example, ever see the Starbucks logo? What's *that*? Still, some connection will be helpful.

• A logo that's based on letters or numbers. These will probably be your company initials, although if your business name contains a number, you could use that. For example, a logo for a business called "77 Landsdowne Street" could be "77."

3. Draft a sketch

Even if you're hiring someone, draft it yourself. Even a rough idea will help. And keep it simple. You don't want details that may not translate into a great web design or have so much nuance you can't reasonably add color.

4. Design the logo

Now, design your logo, working from the simplest form to the most finished, even if you're using clip art or the do-it-yourself wonders of a Mac. If possible, start with black and white, then add color. According to the experts, two-color works best for logos. If you're using words, remember the suggestive quality of fonts. You don't want *Brush Script MT* if you're trying for sassy.

5. Test it

Before settling on a logo, test it. Does it hold up equally well on your website, brochure, and business card? If you have cars or vans, print out a large-scale version and see how it looks on the rear or door. Then, once you're sufficiently enthusiastic about your logo, do a little testing by asking customers and colleagues if they're enthusiastic, too.

When Image Meets Brand

If you have a retail store or an office where clients visit, then you probably know the role this space plays in building your brand. But are you using this space as well as you can to reflect your brand and market your product? Or are you falling into the same old, same old of workplaces supplying similar offerings?

Unless you've really put thought and effort into it, you're probably not maximizing the value of this space. Where you start, though, is another matter and ties directly into your brand.

Aesthetics

Perhaps the best place to start—and one you can control, whether you lease or own—is color. What is the color of your walls? How about the carpeting? Is it dull or bright? Does it reflect other color elements of your brand, like your logo? Not that you need to match exactly, but you certainly don't want to portray your offering as fast-paced and modern and then welcome customers into a sea of beige.

Maybe you've already decided on a color scheme for your interior. Or perhaps you bought furniture at a warehouse where cost and speed of delivery reigned and design was an afterthought. Before you start thinking it's too late to change, think small, as in pictures for the walls, a floor rug (even on top of your wall-to-wall carpet), or even painting the frames.

As for the furniture, rather than rushing into your typical office setup, try thinking of what best suits your brand. Going for a comfortable feel? Try comfortable furniture: oversized chairs, perhaps, and a large coffee table. Going for high tech? Then think sparse and open.

Giveaways

No matter what you do, giveaways are a definite plus. What you give away, though, depends not only on your brand, but your profession. If you're a dentist, lollipops for the kids post-checkup are a definite no.

A great example is my insurance agent. His office is crammed with overflowing bookshelves, papers, and tables loaded with, well, stuff. But like Larsen's Shoes that I mentioned earlier, "the brand," with all it promises, is there. The stuff, which he loads into my arms every time I walk in the door, includes maps, road books, pencils, calendars—all of them with his agency name on it, and amazingly, all of it in some way helpful.

He always greets me personally, too, although he has a receptionist and several employees. The furnishings are old but comfortable, and someone always offers coffee or tea. No question, my insurance agent does not think about brand. But everything from the giveaways to the tagline on his card expresses it: he's the *neighborhood* agent.

Employees

Naturally, you can't pick employees that match your décor. That would be weird. But you can help them support your brand in two ways. One, as you probably know intuitively, is through their dress. Most professional organizations range between professional suit-and-tie attire and casual Fridays all week long. You can really make a statement, though, by having your employees dress in a counter-culture style. The insurance agent I mentioned lets his employees wear jeans, for example, and just about no one wears a tie. Of course, you should only take bold steps when it's prudent.

More important is how your employees treat the customer. You probably know they should be helpful and polite. That's a given, although not everyone in the world follows it. But think about other aspects of your brand. If you're trying to project an image that says "We're the experts!" better make sure your employees know what they're talking about. If you're aiming for the "local folks" appeal, make sure your employees are from the area or intimately familiar with it.

CASE STUDY: THE INSIDE-OUT APPROACH

One of my clients, a small but rapidly growing bank, needed to up their marketing efforts to better compete with an onslaught of competitors. So I conducted focus groups with their employees and managers in true marketing from within fashion. Just about everyone viewed the bank as a friendly, homey sort of place, the anti-corporate institution where people "genuinely care."

Fortunately, this was precisely what their primary clients—burned-out urban professionals—wanted. Unfortunately, you'd never recognize these qualities when you first walked in the door. Their lobby looked like every other bank: a clean, orderly place where a lineup of bored employees waited for customers.

What to do? To start, the bank decided to have a small table with a coffee maker and cookies available all hours. This not only provided a pleasant experience for the customer, but it filled the bank with a slight, unimposing coffee scent that gave a real homey feel. Even better, it encouraged people to sit back and relax as they waited for an account specialist to see them, setting the mood for a long and happy relationship.

As for the tellers, they were given incentives to engage customers, think up ideas about what would make the bank a homier place, and discuss general ways the bank could improve. They memorized new customers' names, learned a bit about their personal lives, and were alerted to their typical transactions. The bank also extended its hours—and its giveaways. As for growth? Since that time, it has opened two new branches.

CASE STUDY: AND THE INSTANT MARKETING FROM WITHIN WINNER IS . . .

Imagine this: Shepherdstown, West Virginia. A Civil War–era relic within commuting distance of Washington, D.C. A genteel town, one part Southern hospitality, one part high-powered D.C. intellectual. So, when Garth Janssen and Lissa Brown opened their coffee shop, they could have created a small-town version of Starbucks or a low-key café. But not Garth and Lissa. That just isn't them. Instead, they marketed from within. Here's what they did:

The name

Garth's parents were driving through Shepherdstown when their dog escaped from the car. They spent the afternoon looking for their lost dog, and in the process discovered Shepherdstown's charm. They liked it so much, they moved in soon after. Hence the name: the Lost Dog. (Oh, about the real dog: they found him.)

The sign

Garth, an artist, designed their logo and sign, which is—no surprise—a dog. This is no corporate hunting hound, though. It's a one-of-a-kind caricature of a big-bellied mutt holding a steaming cup of espresso.

The interior

Garth and Lissa handpicked everything from the furniture—from yard sales—to the wood in the interior. Since they consider beverage-making an art, they positioned the tea and espresso machines so customers could see them. As for the design: paintings from local artists hang on the wall. No Monet imitations here. And the music? Well . . . it's very Lost Dog and rather hard to explain.

The offerings

The first in town to offer espresso. As for the teas? Where do they *get* those teas? They must have a hundred outrageous varieties, but that's not the point. The point is the Lost Dog has its own spin on lots of drinks—even the Chai comes from one of Garth's personal recipes.

The culture

Lost Dog is all about integrity. No corn syrup sweetening the tea; the best ingredients only. They keep the prices affordable, raising the price of drip coffee once in ten years. And their employees are painstakingly trained and have personal accountability for all that occurs under their watch.

The success

In terms of name recognition, ask anyone who's been to Shepherdstown, and they know the Lost Dog. In fact, Lissa claims café owners along the east coast know of it. And visitors to Shepherdstown make a point of stopping in. As for that detail known as profit? They've been making one for a decade, enough to pay their employees and support their family of four.

Section II

Marketing Imperatives

Chapter 4

Ten Imperatives of Instant Marketing Success

If you're going to have a marketing campaign, you must have marketing materials. Everyone knows this, but judging by the quality of marketing material out there, you'd think no one was paying attention. I mean, some of the stuff—actually, *most* of it—is bad. This, by the way, is great news for you. Your marketing material can be worlds better than your competitors' and bring you the response you want.

But to reap those rewards, you had better do ten critical things. We'll return to them throughout the rest of this book—and you should be sure to return to them for the rest of your marketing life.

Imperative 1: It Should Be Useful!

Think of all the business cards you've received in your life. How many are there? Hundreds? Thousands? Now, think of all the cards you have scanned in your computer. Filed in your Rolodex. Kept anywhere in your office. How many is that? Twenty? Thirty? Less? And the brochures? How many of those have you saved for more than an afternoon?

The answer speaks to the number-one challenge business owners face when producing marketing material: how do you get the customer to pay attention to it? And the answer, oft forgot by business owners everywhere, is to give it a purely utilitarian function. Dentists and hairdressers learned this lesson long ago for more immediate and practical reasons: they put the time and date of the appointment on the back of their business card. The customers remember the appointment *and* keep the card, so the next time that tooth aches or the hair grows too low on the brow, they know exactly whom to call.

Giving your marketing material a utilitarian function also insures that your customer will return to your marketing material again and again. Take the Web. Here you have ample opportunities to offer your customer useful—even indispensable—information. You can provide tips or a spoken lesson every week or two that your customer will eagerly access. Only remember: update the site regularly. Freshness is the key to having frequent visitors!

If you happen to be in retail or manufacturing, where lessons of this sort may be impractical, think about the other marketing materials you dispense. Have a brochure? Your hours of operation are helpful, but how about putting safety tips on the back—perfect for the workplace bulletin board. If you're in the security business, how about a list of emergency numbers on the back of your brochure, business cards, or anywhere they'll fit. This will enhance your visibility, ensure the customer equates your brand with safety, and come in handy in an emergency.

Naturally, you can boost your exposure with giveaways, too. And I am not talking about Tootsie Roll pops or oversized erasers that might get a laugh but end up in the trash. Pens and pencils are okay, but face the small-object reality—the print is usually too tiny for anyone to see, affordable varieties tend to be cheap and the customers unlikely to value them, and they're just the right size to slip behind a couch pillow or roll on the floor, never to be seen again.

Instead, try for something *really* useful. Calendars are an all-time favorite, and as we'll discuss in greater detail, with computer programs you can do it yourself, no problem. I have a calendar from the West Virginia Extension Service posted right by my garden door, alerting customers like me not only of national holidays, but also the correct time to plant my garden, purchase lime, and countless other details most of us don't know or remember.

Unusual giveaways with your name and number on them can prove even more beneficial than the standard ones, just as long as there's a *direct* connection to your business. For example, the art supply and framing store down the street gives away yardsticks. I've had mine for years. And the insurance agent I mentioned earlier gives away great road maps. True, he's an agent and probably couldn't afford the upscale merchandise if his parent company didn't send it. But there's plenty out there that you *can* afford and that your customer will appreciate.

Imperative 2: Use Marketing Smarts!

Business owners often produce marketing material simply because everyone else does. Resist this impulse! Be smart about what you produce and how much time you devote to developing new material. Here are some pointers that will help:

• Create an image and style of word use that you can easily duplicate from one marketing piece to another. Have a great logo and put it everywhere—your brochure, your website, and anywhere else it needs to go. Make sure you can easily duplicate the style of your business cards on your stationery and website.

• Consider what marketing pieces you really need. Let's assume you're on a limited budget. You need to consider the functional aspect of your marketing materials. If you're an organizational consultant or researcher, you may produce a newsletter highlighting your recent projects or findings. And naturally, you'll post it on the Web. But do you really need to send emails to your busy customers saying it's out there? It may only clutter their inboxes and annoy them.

• Think volume. One key marketing strategy is determining how you can reach as many of your primary customers as possible. So, you want marketing material that's sure to reach them—and nothing else. Lots of consulting firms, for example, spend boatloads of employee time (and therefore money) writing white papers. These ads/articles/exposés may make the author feel important and knowledgeable, but reality check: who reads them? Better to develop a breathtaking presentation for a conference or a short article, or even better, a tip sheet your customer can really use.

Imperative 3: Focus On the Customer—Not You, Your Business, Your Employees, or Anything Else

Your customers don't care about you. Or your employees. Or your business philosophy. Not even how many years you've been around. What they *do* care about is how all these matters affect them—what we call the customer-focus.

Say you're writing a brochure for Business Supply Services, an office supply store that is trying to compete with the Big Guys. What they lack in pricing (they're more expensive) they make up for in customer service. Now, they're rolling out a new concept: they've partnered with a leading insurance company to offer business coverage with representatives right in the store. Their target: small-business owners who may not be insured.

Note how the first sample focuses on Business Supply Services and the other focuses on the customer.

BSS: Business Supply Services now offers affordable insurance coverage for small businesses.

Customer: Now, you can get affordable insurance for your small business without adding an extra trip to your schedule.

Here's another example:

BSS: Our customer service is unmatched in the industry. Our staff knows office products and is available to answer questions.

Customer: You will receive unmatched customer service from staff who know office products and will readily answer your questions.

The best connection in this regard is a direct connection: the written equivalent of a handshake, a good laugh, drinking a frothy beer together at a pub. Well, maybe not *quite* that direct. Here are a few more pointers:

• Use language that makes the customer feel comfortable. You don't want to talk *at* them, but *to* them. Even if you're writing to a fellow industry professional, lean toward the calm, friendly language you'd use at a dinner party and not a boardroom presentation. So in a line like this: "Our research will assist you in the determination of what results transpire in actual events that occur when following normal procedural actions . . ." you're no longer one person addressing another, but a company talking to the air. Instead, try saying: "With the information in our research, you'll be able to predict the results you'll get when following normal procedures."

• Discard anything that does not directly benefit the customer. An accounting firm I know produced a brochure that best illustrates this classic mistake. The cover showed a picture of the CPA and his staff, in what looked like a holiday greeting snapshot. All nice, friendly people, but I need to see them because . . . ? Then, the copy gave a chronology of the firm, dating back to when most customers were probably toddlers. "Back then, we were called Data Processing Professionals . . ." the brochure read. No one—and I repeat *no one*—cares, which doesn't matter, since the customer probably didn't make it past the photo anyway.

• Use the second person "you." This is possible 100 percent of the time in your marketing materials. That doesn't mean you must use the second person in every sentence, but readers should know you're speaking directly to them. For example, I just picked up a great brochure for a yoga retreat in Mexico. The opening line: "Float through winter on the turquoise waters of the Mexican Caribbean." No question, the customers know the message is directed at them.

The Exceptions

Avoid the second person if you're going to insult your reader by doing so.

Let's return to Business Supply Services one last time. Say the company is writing a flyer about a recent survey revealing that small-business owners have big misconceptions about office insurance.

The point of the flyer: address their misconceptions, position the company as a small-business expert, and encourage customers to sign up for insurance at one of its locations. Of course, you can't say, "*You* have misconceptions . . ." because they may be insulted. This, in turn, breaks an unspoken cardinal marketing rule: don't insult your customer. Instead, focus on those other poor dolts, the ones from the survey. That way, you address your customers' misconceptions without insulting them, dispel their myths, and get them to buy the insurance. The typical approach goes like this:

"A recent survey reveals that over 65 percent of small-business owners have serious misconceptions about insurance coverage for their office."

Instead, try this:

"Are you aware of the benefits of insuring your business? Amazingly, over 65 percent of small-business owners have serious misconceptions about what insurance coverage really means. Here's what you need to know . . ."

Promise Results: Look at any ad out there. The gazillion-dollar copywriters know you'll only respond if the copy immediately and indisputably promises a result. Weight-loss or muscle-building programs are the most obvious examples, with their promise, either spoken or suggested, that "this could be you!" But just about every ad promises something, often overstepping the bounds by linking perfume to a better love life and a car to a better career.

QUICK Tip

Show the Benefits: We talked about word use, but how can the visual component of your marketing piece accentuate the benefits your customer will experience? The answer: in photos, graphics, and everything else, display what they get, not what you do.

For example, I have an architect friend whose specialty is designing or rehabilitating schools. He's much better off showing images of the schools he's created, especially with happy schoolchildren going in and out the doors, than the standard snapshot of people sitting around a table discussing plans.

Imperative 4: Accentuate the Customer Benefits

In Imperative 3, I said your marketing effort must focus on the customers. Let's add a caveat to that idea: it must focus on how they'll benefit from your offering. Think about the old customer service concept. Sure, the customer service reps will help you every time you walk into the store. But so what? I mean, the idea is great, but how will it make the customer's life easier or more productive? The answer would read this way: "You can get informed advice from our staff to help you purchase the best products at the lowest possible price."

Perhaps the most glaring glitch in the benefits approach comes from the "We love you, we care about you; that's why we're selling you our product/service/everything else." Face it, most businesses have a hard time pulling off a lovey-dovey approach because it crosses the work/personal relationship line. The customer knows this and knows your real motivation is *not* to express love for them, but to make a profit. So the message sounds phony. Take this familiar-sounding line:

"Business Supply Services cares about you and your business. That's why we want you to know the truth about insurance coverage."

Better to focus on the customer:

"Your business may be vulnerable in ways you may not expect. That's why you should know the truth about insurance coverage."

Of course, you can always state the benefit directly:

"Make sure your business is fortified from potential losses by learning . . ."

Imperative 5: Use a Catch-and-Keep Approach

A recent study led by Carleton University in Ottawa, Canada, revealed a startling fact: the average person takes fifty milliseconds—that's less time than it takes you to blink your eye—to form an opinion about a website. That's an impression that sticks. The study said there's a "halo effect" where a visitor's opinion of the rest of the site—and your offering—is formed by that first impression.

All this proves what marketing professionals have known for a long time: you must get the customer's attention, instantly and completely, or they're gone. With visuals, this means finding the perfect design, photo, or cartoon that fuels an instant feeling, from humor to concern. With words, this means getting them to focus on one or two key words, but no more.

Once you get going, *always* start every new segment of your text with quick, interesting, funny, alarming, or otherwise blood-quickening words. That means the headline on your brochure, the first words of your direct mail piece, the subject line of your email, and the home page of your website must be *sharp*. Then, don't let your lively style drop! Follow through on the remaining segments.

QUICK Tip

Never Ever:

• State obvious information. You're secretly signaling the message is irrelevant, insincere, or boring. Say no to obvious. Say yes to fresh, funny, fascinating, new.

• Use sentence openers like "As you know . . ." "As most people know . . ." or similar phrases. This signals the information is unnecessary and probably boring.

• Start with a spicy, pithy, or otherwise interesting opening, then offer up the word-use equivalent of yesterday's beer in the subsequent paragraphs.

Imperative 6: Keep the Word Use Clear and Clean

It may seem silly even to mention that your marketing material should be well-written. *Naturally*, you think. *Why state the obvious?* But remarkably, most marketing material is pretty bad. I'm not just referring to copy that small businesses with small budgets create; I mean everyone! The language wanders, the grammar does its own thing, so to speak, and the message is basically a wash.

By cleaning up the style, you'll have noticeably better material, particularly if you plan to distribute it at conferences or place it in racks where people will compare. But a word of caution: if you write the copy yourself, have someone check it. Make sure that someone is a good writer, too, with an eye for problems. If you hire copywriters, check their writing closely. Remember what I said a moment ago: most marketing material is pretty poorly written and there's no reason why this marketing expert should produce anything different.

Here are the items you should check for:

Correct Grammar

Sometimes the best copy has errors that even schoolchildren know to avoid. A common one is noun-verb agreement: "The best way for children to get what they need are to ask for it." It should read: "The best way for children to get what they need is to ask for it." Of course, potential grammar problems are limitless, so as I said, check carefully.

Passive Voice

The passive voice is a typical problem in marketing material. Some authors think it sounds more professional and convincing. Others just plunk it in without even realizing it. Regardless, the passive voice creates an artificial sound that's deadly to your marketing voice and can even interfere with the meaning you're trying to convey. Here are four instances of the passive voice. Avoid them all.

• **Don't separate the subject and the verb.** You learned about this in high school: "You will be immediately helped by one of our customer services reps." Notice that the subject, "customer service rep," occupies the back end of the sentence, after the verb. Instead, say: "One of our customer sales reps will immediately help you." The difference may seem slight in one sentence, but when repeated over and over, this mistake adds lots of extra words, convoluting sentence structure and making for a boring tone.

• **Don't leave out the subject.** This problem will leave *you* out of the picture altogether, when you should be starring in it. You know this problem well, I'm sure, from sentences that read: "All phone calls will be answered within twenty-four hours" or "Any problems and the cost of your entire system will be refunded." Who's answering these calls? And who's refunding the money? The sentence doesn't tell you. So here are the rewrites: "Our specialists will answer your phone calls within twenty-four hours" and "We will refund the cost of your entire system if you have problems."

• **Don't disguise your verbs.** Stay away from sentences with verbs posing as nouns, like this one: "The development phase typically takes only two weeks." Instead, get that action in there, and write: "Typically we only need two weeks to develop the infrastructure."

• **Don't use empty actors.** Okay, I admit that this one isn't so bad, but it's not so great, either. That's where you say: "There are six steps that you can take. It is important that you take all of them." The "there are" and "it is" contain verbs, but "there" and "it" really aren't the actors. Here's the rewrite: "Be sure to take all six steps."

Cohesion

This is the order of your information. Make sure you don't just plunk your points on the page; see that one flows logically to the next. Even in brochures or those short direct mail pieces where the individual paragraphs may seem only loosely related, have a master plan that holds everything together. Try using numbers. For example: "Seven Reasons Why Mason's Motor Oil Is Right for Your Car," or take a direction, such as smallest item to largest.

Tone

Make sure all your marketing material is 100 percent—yes, that's right, 100 percent—jargon-free. I don't care if you *are* an engineer, software developer, or health plan expert. Jargon shrivels up the tone of any marketing piece, no matter how jazzy the graphics. And keep it friendly, accessible, and generally upbeat.

Conciseness

It's true, less is more. But concise is slightly different. Supply your customer with all the points they must know, but only use necessary words. Here's what you do: write the marketing piece, or review the finished product if someone wrote it for you. Then, get out your red pen (or use your computer's track changes program) and cross out any filler. Be especially aware of phrases like "In the event that" and "Due to the fact that," and substitute one word such as "if" and "because." When you're finished, smooth out the sentence structure—with all those missing words, you're bound to find some holes.

QUICK Tip

Imitate the Experts: Go to the magazine rack at your local bookstore and flip through the pages. Notice the tight, lively word use. The active voice. And the way section after section flows smoothly. Remember this when you develop your marketing materials. While the marketing–magazine connection may seem sketchy at best, it isn't. Magazines know the style the readers like best, and it applies to everything—even the most routine proposals!

Imperative 7: Use White Space Wisely

White space does more than provide a break to the customer's eye. It's essential. Here are just a few benefits:

• *Creates a friendly feel.* Customers frequently misinterpret that wall of ink in long paragraphs as an unfriendly, aloof, or otherwise hostile sentiment, no matter what the word use.

• *Looks like less.* Say you have fifteen lines in a paragraph. The customer immediately perceives this as something as long as an excerpt from *War and Peace*. But divide it into three bite-sized paragraphs of five lines, and it's almost edible.

- *Gives the customer's eye room to wander.* In the process, he might jump from paragraph to paragraph, especially if you have bullets, callouts, and sidebars. Wandering, by the way, is a good thing. In most cases, the only other option is to quit reading.

Perhaps the best reason to use white space, though, is that every web page, presentation, and coupon require it. Once you do add information, remember that customers want easy-to-read, easy-to-see nuggets of information. But beware of some typical hazards.

For example, brochures, presentations (PowerPoint and others), and other longer text documents frequently suffer from bullet mania. That's where you see page after page of bullets, making the piece look like a connect-the-dots game without the numbers. The overuse of bullets creates the very monotony they were intended to break.

Another malady typical of web marketing messages: pages that provide interesting visuals but little text and even less useful text. The visitor has to click through the site, searching for basic information. The site is breaking a cardinal rule: never make the reader work for information. Instead, place critical points where the customer can instantly see them. A key point in the far left corner? Don't think so, unless you don't have any other text on the page, and not a whole lot of image. Key point positioned near center screen? Better. Much better.

Another space problem evolved about ten or fifteen years ago. You see it in brochures, newsletters, and websites. You can tell the designer was going for a high-energy feel, but instead created busy, chaotic images so intense the visitor's eye has nowhere to focus. Every page of every piece is loaded with so many images the customer feels dizzy just looking at them. As for the written message? It's buried in an avalanche of shapes and color and the customer never actually sees it. Make sure your designers understand that it's the message of the site—not the visual impact—that's important.

Alert!

Watching Websites: Take a virtual walk through the Web and look at how some of the big guys manage space. One of my favorites is Nike (www.nike.com). Their website manages to have exceptional speed and energy without lots of clutter.

Imperative 8: Apply Font Savvy

So many fonts, so little time to use them. They support the mood you want to express, injecting **importance**, *emphasis*, and <u>visibility</u> to your points. Of course, you could say: *importance*, <u>emphasis</u>, and **visibility**, but no matter.

Besides, fonts add variety, which is always a good thing. In the old days, for example, you used quotation marks for things people said. Now, you can replace quotation marks with italics in some cases and keep them in others, such as a call-out in your newsletter or brochure. Even better, fonts create personality, independent of words, content, and sentence structure. Vive la difference:

Come to our <u>**BIG SALE!!**</u> **DON'T** miss <u>OUT!!</u>

and

Come to our big sale . . . Don't miss out!

Naturally, those font additives bring visual dimension to your message—great for the ever-longing-for-entertainment reader.

So, with all these pluses, could font possibly have a downside? Uh-huh. That's when the **bolds**, *italics*, large letters, and other font variations appear cheap or gratuitous, much like blue nail polish at an upscale dinner party. Besides, you risk alienating the customer who gets distracted into oblivion. Equally bad, the font can distract you—the writer—from using powerful and nicely controlled words, instead letting you rely on this cheap substitute for meaning.

Imperative 9: Consider the "Love at Fifth Sight" Principle

Love at fifth sight should be the mantra of anyone producing marketing material. Customers, especially prospective customers, probably won't remember you the first time they see your brochure or ad, or even the second time. Maybe the third time, perhaps the fourth, but the fifth . . . now they've *got* to remember! How you reach them, as we'll discuss soon, depends on your customer, your location, and obviously, your offering. But one thing's for sure: you need a mixture of approaches to make your marketing effort work.

That means you must support every marketing piece you send with several others. For example, say you're running an ad in your local paper. You can't run an ad and expect results. You can't run thirty ads and expect results, either. But thirty ads, direct mail material, banners in front of your site, and phone calls to key primary customers, and you're all set.

Imperative 10: Avoid *Anything* Boring, Especially Clichés, the Anti-Brand!

Most marketing material suffers from one resounding malady: it's boring. Really boring. And in this day of speed, dazzle, and information overload, that's a fierce problem. With word use, whether in ads, TV spots, or newsletters, your greatest enemies are clichés. And trust me, everyone uses them in marketing material, although common sense and good taste indicate you should do otherwise. Before you read further, take this vow: never, ever use clichés in any marketing material or presentation, by phone or Web, live or recorded.

Here are a few clichés to watch for. They float to the page, so meaningless they're anemic. And vacuous? They're the dumb blondes of marketing material. Here goes:

Leader

Trust me, every large company and plenty of small ones claim they're a leader in something. We have so many leaders in the world, it's amazing we have any followers. You've seen the claims. They litter just about every brochure, business card, ad, and website, saying something like this:

See why we're a leading auto repair specialist . . .

A recognized leader in home care . . .

Today, our combination of high-quality products and superior customer service makes us a leader in the industry.

Assume for a minute the leader line has a fragment of value. These questions still linger: What is it leading? Why should the prospective customer care if the company is a leader? What does "leadership" have to do with the product or service it offers?

Needs

This word is so common and totally ambiguous; it doesn't matter what industry or region, or even what's for sale. See if you can spot the industries in the following samples:

Someone can assist you in making decisions for your changing needs.

Meeting all your Italian American needs.

Help us meet your specific needs.

Don't know? Let me tell you.

1. Insurance company. In fact, just about every insurance company has a similar line taking unfortunate prominence on their website. This is especially toxic for an industry struggling to break through the boring and insipid image most people ascribe to it and became somehow human, jovial, and real.

2. The little Italian grocery store in Gloucester, Massachusetts, which really couldn't meet all of anyone's Italian American needs. Their supplies were so low you couldn't even make a snack from them.

3. This is a health insurance company. A big one with plenty of money

to invest in a great website. Unfortunately, this takes center spot on the home page.

Another problem with "needs" is that it sounds disingenuous—far removed from the customers' thinking. Look, whoever says, "Hmm, I guess my insurance needs have changed. . . ."? And when do you ever say to your spouse, "Honey, you need to consider your vacation needs"? You get the idea.

Commitment

Most marketing writers feel obliged, for reasons I have never understood, to use the "C" word. You know, commitment. It's meaningless, and far more interesting when concerning marriage ceremonies or mental institutions than business transactions. Besides, who cares about a commitment? It's symbolic and promissory; customers want the real thing. So, commit yourself to avoiding the "C" word; then, don't use it.

24/7

We know you're somehow available 24/7. That's the point of the Web. Otherwise, we'd only have offices that close at 5 p.m. and answering services so we could get back to customers later. The only thing worse than "24/7" when you're talking time is something like this:

> Ready to help you, 24/7. You can access information anytime, day
> or night, 24 hours a day, 7 days a week, 365 days a year, even
> Christmas . . .

All right already! Of course, if you have live, walking and breathing customer service reps in the office day and night, that's a different story. How many places, aside from your local hospital or convenience store, can claim that? If you must indulge in the 24/7 routine, go ahead, but please, find new ways to say it.

Tailored

These days, everyone promises services that are "tailored" to meet your needs, requirements, and so on. The "tailored" word would be great, too, if everyone else didn't make that promise. But in most cases, that's the very purpose of, say, dress sizes, proposals, a pre-program analysis, and marketing research. In fact, you'd be hard-pressed to find anything that *isn't* tailored! Otherwise, you might end up selling bathing suits to Eskimos. Find a better, more specific way to highlight your customer service.

Only a Click Away

Aside from being a cliché, it's not true. You don't click once; you probably click five or six times, at least, and have to enter all sorts of passwords and credit card numbers. So forget it.

From the Comfort of Your Home

Cliché? Yes, cliché. Besides, who says their homes are comfortable? If they have three or four kids, their homes definitely aren't comfortable. More likely, they're chaotic. Maybe they're just too hassled to leave.

Beating Clichés: Every time you yearn to use a cliché, stop yourself, take a deep breath, and think up something specific. What evidence do you have that you're committed to optimal customer service? Are all your employees certified somehow? Do you keep longer hours than everyone else in the business? If you meet their needs, how so? Do you offer unusual services because of your clients' circumstances? If you own a restaurant, do you accommodate specific dietary needs? Focus on the specifics that make your business stand out and the clichés will melt away.

QUICK Tip

The Exception Proves the Rule: The only time to say "yes" to clichés and tired expressions is when you use clichés *as* clichés, having fun with them, and sympathizing with your customers. In a sense, it sets you apart, creating an "us not them" relationship. Here are some examples:

Through this program, we're proving that our "commitment" to lower prices can be translated into "numbers."

Sure, everyone offers online services 24/7: but when we say "24/7" we mean something better . . .

Saying we're a leader means more than saying we're one of the oldest companies in Howardsville. It means we take risks. Find new solutions. We're really ahead of the crowd. Here are just a few examples . . .

Alert!

Marketing Your Marketing: Beware of the "marketing your marketing" trap. This is one of the most underestimated marketing expenses of all. Here are two scenarios that will undoubtedly sound familiar:

• You build a website. It's attractive, user-friendly, and slick—boy, is it slick! Only one problem: no one's visiting it. That's rather like cooking a gourmet dinner and having it sit on the table, untouched, as it grows cold. So, naturally enough, you have to market your website through search engines, tags on your other marketing material, and more. And all this requires more time and, of course, more money.

• You plan an open house where customers can have a little wine, a little cheese, and plenty of tip sheets, giveaways, and other information. But you have to market this event with invitations, announcements, news releases, and signs, and you're broke before the first customer walks through the door!

So, as you budget for marketing, don't forget this hidden and altogether real expense.

Record What You've Learned

Turn to Worksheet 3 (page 228). You'll find all the items here in a valuable checklist. Use it for every marketing piece your business produces!

Chapter 5

Get the Right Response

Plenty of people develop plenty of marketing material (often at great expense) because . . . well, because they do. They write the copy themselves or hire someone at hundreds of dollars a pop. And sometimes, the results are great—brochures attractive as postcards, websites that dazzle.

Only they forget to address one critical question that makes the difference between marketing material that brings in business and copy that's nice to look at. And that issue?

The specific response they want from their marketing effort. Granted, the response you probably want has dollar signs around it. But reality tells us that's simply not how marketing works. So many other factors are involved, among them timing, desire, and cost.

So, what other actions are you trying to elicit from your customers? Name it. In case you're stumped, here's a list:

- Call your sales department to order a product
- Accept the call when your sales rep calls
- Prefer you over the competition
- Order a product online
- Request a proposal
- Supply information
- Look for your ad in the newspaper
- Refer your business to other people
- Agree with your view—particularly about industry-related matters
- Support your view
- Show up for an event
- Buy several items, not one or two
- Sign up to join your organization
- Sign up their friends
- Call their representative on your behalf
- Remember your brand
- Like your brand

Emotional Appeal

What is the secret to getting the right response from your marketing material? Focus on the emotion, and not the intellect, in your pitch, no matter whether you're saying it, showing it, or writing it. The benefits we talked about in the last chapter are critical here. So is establishing a real "feel" for your message: excitement, comfort, rebelliousness. Naturally, this is *always* consistent with your brand.

Here are a few points you must remember:

- You can process ten thousand times more information with the eye than the ear. So while sound rings true—and can support the visual—

don't use it alone. If you're giving a presentation or hosting a training session as part of your marketing campaign, use a flip chart to outline your points. PowerPoint presentations are okay for large audiences who can't see your writing, but they can also distract the customer, have limited (okay, *no*) visual appeal, and can overshadow your presence.

• Your customer's first response is visceral, which means that first fifty milliseconds must shake them, body and soul. That, of course, triggers the all-important emotion that sends them your way.

• While delicious visuals get a consuming response, language has a more enduring and substantive effect, so use them both wisely.

• Mixing visuals, language, and sound triggers numerous sensations, and as the saying goes, three are better than one—but the three must work harmoniously together.

• Keep it simple. Don't overdose customers with messages. Think of your primary customers, your primary offering, and the primary response you want from them.

• Sentence structure is your key, and it's the most underestimated tool to getting a visceral response in everything from emails to direct mails.

Sentence Structure Secrets

Let's linger a bit on sentence structure. Short, quick sentences give your material an excited, even urgent sound, perfect for innovative, fast-moving firms. The longer your sentences, the more relaxed the feeling you project. So for urgent-sounding messages, use short sentences. For sweet and human ones, make them longer:

Urgent: Don't delay! Purchase one today!

Sweet and human: You can start enjoying one today!

You probably noticed the words changed, too. And, yes, you need those words to match the sentence length. "Enjoy," for example, makes you think of sunny vacations or other pleasantries. "Purchase," on the other hand, is more businesslike. As for "start," this word has a slowness to it when compared to the abrupt alliteration of "don't delay."

Here are some other feelings you can capture, working on this theme:

Excitement

- Short sentences with strong, immediate verbs
- Bullets
- Clear, quick order

You may need to project excitement frequently, occasionally, or in core places within a piece. The excitement could be over something positive—even riveting—like a local football game you're sponsoring, a community event, a sale, or a new product. Or it can be negative, like critical steps the reader must take to avoid an emergency. Good or bad, the strategy is the same. Try to convey the breathlessness of excitement using short sentences or a sentence with plenty of starts and pauses. Don't be afraid to jolt the reader or be abrupt. That's the point, isn't it?

Here are two examples—one about good and one about bad circumstances.

Good: Football game

The crowd roars. The action begins. And the fans from Biltmore Vineyards are in the stands, cheering the loudest.

Bad: An accident

Wheels squeak. A rush of metal heads your way and *bam*! A massive thud. Yes, you've been in an accident. You gather your wits, but what to do next?

Calm

- Longer sentences
- Clear, orderly transitions

Ask anyone with Birkenstocks and a meditative look—calm takes time. You need to relax, breathe, go with the flow . . . and that's precisely how to project calm in your sentences. Not boring or wordy. But . . . sigh . . . calm. . . . Remember that previous example about an accident?

Notice the difference:

> So you've been in an accident. Take a breath, relax, and let yourself calm down. Perhaps you can still hear the wheels squeak and see the metal heading your way before the accident's thud. Now you need to gather your wits and decide what to do next.

Humor

- Fragments, single-word sentences, and questions
- True and false statements and other devices

The essence of humor is keeping the readers off guard, surprising them. And it's easy to surprise a reader long accustomed to long sentences, clear transitions, and predictable paragraph length. Be creative, playful, and fun, and play around with words, too. Okay, you may not get a guffaw, but you can still project humor.

> Better service and lower prices? Huh? Is that what those companies are really saying? Take a peek behind the words. You won't believe your eyes.

Seriousness

- Complete sentences
- More compound structure
- Less variety of sentence length

If it's serious, it's got to be direct: no fuss, muss, or bother. That means your sentences shouldn't be too long, but they also shouldn't be so short they sound ludicrously urgent. Use complex sentences, start strong, and place verbs in plain view. Here's an example:

> You may be getting fooled by companies claiming to provide better service and lower prices. So be sure to examine what they're really saying to truly understand their claims.

Nefarious Outreach Checklist: You want to prompt your customer to take an action—otherwise, there's no reason to develop or send a marketing piece. However, you are *not* trying to manipulate the customer into liking or buying your offering. Encouraging him? Absolutely. That's the point behind marketing in the first place, right? You don't market a product so customers will buy someone else's brand. However, manipulation is different from encouragement and has nefarious undertones. If you're insecure about your own intentions, run through this Nefarious Outreach Checklist:

Write "yes" or "no" beside each of the items in this checklist:

✔   I'm not really sure my customers will benefit from my product/service but hey, I know they'll buy it.

✔   Actually, my product isn't anything like what I'm describing, but that's not the point. The point is that the customer thinks it is.

✔   If customers react the way I want them to, they'll go broke.

✔   If customers react the way I want them to, they'll break into hives.

✔   What I'm suggesting would be illegal if I worded it a different way.

✔   I want customers to take certain actions, although they better not know why they take the action.

✔   My message preys on customers' low self-esteem.

If you answered "yes" to one or more items on this list, better get out of the business. If not, just make sure the good deal you're touting really is a good deal and the action you provoke really will benefit the person who's doing it.

Section III

The Instant Marketing Supply Kit

Chapter 6

Signature Materials

Basically, signature materials are the pieces that exclusively represent *you*. They instantly acquaint your customer with your brand, your offering, and your value proposition. You'll need each of these at some point in the earliest stages of your marketing effort, so put them high on your priority list.

Business Cards

Whether you own a retail shop, consulting practice, or manufacturing plant, business cards are a must. They tell customers that you're professional, give them the essentials about your business, and last longer than a handshake or conversation at a meeting.

Cost

Business cards range from about fifty dollars for the whole shebang (if you get a software package) to thousands of dollars (if you have an image consultant or professional graphics designer do them). Even if you're tight on funds, don't scrimp here; your business card will surely be one among many on your customers' desks, and you want it to compete.

Use

Naturally, your business cards tell customers the basics about who you are, what you do, and how they can find you. Bring your business cards everywhere: to every meeting, conference, and family vacation. Yes, I did say family vacation! How many times have you sat around a swimming pool and discovered that the stranger next to you is interested in—or even desperately needs—your service? This the perfect time to hand that person your card (get her phone number, while you're at it).

Depending on your business, your cards can also serve as an ad. For example, if you operate a day care center or massage therapy practice, you can always pin your card on bulletin boards in places your customers frequent, like the children's section of your local library, or your health food store. Beware of posting them in places where they'll get soiled or fall down. You want to look as clean and professional as possible.

To sweeten the business card exchange, consider tastefully attaching a giveaway to your card or vice versa. If you're attending a conference during the holidays, tie small candy canes around your cards and put them in a basket at your display. If you offer tips of some sort, attach your card to the front page, making sure the header on your tip sheet is clear. Or attach a coupon with a limited-time offer. But make sure the giveaway, whether it's a meeting time with you or a product, has real value. The customer, accustomed to overdosing on self-serving information from businesses, will appreciate the difference.

What to Do

Your business card should probably be the first component in your marketing supply kit. The look and feel of your business card should then be reflected in everything you add. Start by determining a look that excites you even after you've handed out your three-thousandth card. If you already have a business card, make sure it's in your comfort zone. If not, review the following steps and make adjustments as you need them.

• **Refine your logo**. By now, you should have a logo and tagline. If not, this is the time to do it. Remember, you have plenty of options where logos are concerned. You can make one yourself, create one from the thousands of possibilities available through clip art, or hire a professional.

• **Pick the right design.** You can choose from countless designs, from web programs to the marketing packages we talked about earlier. Or head for your local copy shop. Most have a seasoned business card expert on hand, ready to give advice. Regardless, make sure the card isn't cluttered, the tagline is visible, and the logo, while important, doesn't hog center stage. Finally, make sure the design matches your brand. Remember those adjectives you wrote in the last chapter. If they included "sturdy," "reliable," and "strong," you certainly shouldn't go for anything with soft or rounded lines.

• **Choose the right paper.** While the paper may not seem like a huge issue, it is. Go for something that's professional and doesn't even hint that you're using anything in the same family as ordinary typing paper. A laid stock is always good, although you may want something glossier. It's easy to figure out how brand fits in here: the sturdy, reliable, and strong product shouldn't get a high-gloss finish. Having said that, make sure your paper doesn't overshadow the rest of your card. Make it too heavy or glossy, or have lettering that rises so high off the paper it could be Braille, and the customer gets distracted.

- **Include relevant information.** You know you need your name, phone numbers, and email and physical addresses, but don't forget your website address. This is a great way to publicize that you're professional enough to have one, and it increases the likelihood that your customer will look favorably upon you.

- **Think utilitarian.** Remember the utilitarian purpose we discussed earlier? Well, the back of your business card, all too often left empty, is the perfect place to give the customer something practical and useful. You can list tips and driving directions to your office. If you're an accountant, list important tasks the customer should remember to complete before April 15. While the printing may take a little longer and cost a little more, the likelihood that your customer will keep your card is that much stronger.

- **Build in time.** If you're in a hurry, beware. My local OfficeMax required two weeks to create business cards and quantity was no matter. And since they contract out, they were inflexible about timing. I opted for a franchise owned by a couple in my community instead. They agreed to get them back within a week. Sorry to say, they apparently ran out of ink, because the week stretched to ten business days, when, alas, the product had a glaring problem: no phone number. Another week passed until I finally had them. This example illustrates that you should plan on waiting if you send your cards out—and don't wait until days before that conference you're attending to order them.

Alert!

What Not to Do: I heard a story on the news the other day about a drug dealer who decided to print up business cards and market his (illegal) trade. The card showed two men in a street fight, one punching the other in the face. The logo read: "If you want a hit, just call the boss," the dealer's name and phone number dutifully beneath it. Two narcotics agents took the hint, called the guy to place an order, and arrested him soon after.

QUICK Tip

Business Card Alternative: Rather than hand out the old-fashioned paper variety, consider giving your customer a CD-ROM. The cost ranges from $2.50 apiece if you want a small quantity (say, twenty or thirty) to under a dollar if you stock up on a thousand or more. Companies that develop the CDs usually need a month or so to produce them. If you're in the entertainment business, the idea is perfect. In manufacturing, maybe not. But if you're tempted, remember Imperative 1 and give it a utilitarian function. Cool information about your business is just not enough.

Photos

If you own a business that relies heavily on you, place a headshot of you high on your priority list. It belongs on your website, beside your bio on the "Who's Who" page, in your press kit if you have one, and other places we'll discuss in a minute.

As far as photos of your product or workplace for your website or brochures, if you're selling a concrete item such as clothing or computers, or have a hotel, retreat, or theme park, you definitely need pictures. They will go up on your website, will enliven your brochure, and may be useful if the local paper decides to feature your company. But if you have street appeal, meaning a sign and an attractive window display, the photo should sink lower on your priority list. Also, keep in mind those Imagery Dos and Don'ts we talked about in chapter 3.

Cost

I hate to admit this, but when I got my photo, I paid a professional $300. This, by the way, was a good deal compared to some of the other photographers I called. But that was in Washington, D.C., and with the high demand for photos from all those politicians running around, the price was bound to be steep. Fortunately, most professional photographers are less expensive, running around $80 for a headshot.

Use

Remember, in the end, people buy from other people. If you provide a professional service, including consulting, training, and teaching, the more face time you have with the customer the better. Where your picture belongs and where a picture of your business belongs, though, is a different matter.

Let's start with you. As I mentioned, have a small photo of yourself (and even of key employees, depending on how great a role they play in your business) on your website beside your bio. Keep the photo handy for your press kit if you have one, and for a newspaper that might be featuring your company or a milestone event at your business.

While most will happily send a photographer to do the job, trust me, you're better off choosing your own. You can control the image *and* know the result will be clean, clear, and worth clipping.

If you plan to give talks, conduct seminars, or provide presentations, you can blow up your picture so it suits a small poster that will announce the name of the talk, the time, and so on. Most event planners will make the poster for you; you provide the photo. Whether you plan to put your face on your brochure is another matter. If you do, you need to have each copy professionally printed or the image will be blurred or otherwise substandard. This, in turn, means added expense.

As for a product? Because customers are buying a concrete item, a great photo will tease them into wanting it. So yes, get those photos into your brochure, website, ads, coupons, you name it—but, as I've said, make sure those pictures are good.

What to Do

If your impulse is to run out to your nearest photo booth, forget it. The price might be right, but the product will be wrong. And obviously, a Kodak snapped in the backyard is out of the question. As for Sears or one of the less expensive department stores, they're great for photos of the kids with a background of Santa's reindeer, but for a professional look, probably not. My vote is to go with a pro, but here are a few points to remember.

To start, give yourself time. My trip to the photographer in D.C. took around three hours, with a return visit of another hour to review the actual pictures. During the first visit, a makeup artist did my face, but the treatment was not exactly Mary Kay. Purple on the cheekbones, so much pancake makeup I thought my pores would close up, and eyebrows the color (and consistency) of coal. Once the shooting began, he told me to sit at such bizarre angles that I thought I was playing a one-person game of Twister.

This photographer also said I should bring three changes of clothes, and he snapped me in all three. Good thing, too. Although all were business clothes, their different color and style changed the impression of the picture. As for background, white screens of various hues. No sky, no office images, no fan blowing my hair.

Of course, another photographer I saw had a remarkably different approach. Makeup? "We have a mirror in the back," he said. Background? He had everything from fluffy clouds to a sheet of gray. Timing? About thirty minutes. Change of clothing? Huh? The result? Okay. Not exceptional, but certainly usable and affordable. Whether you go expensive highbrow or low-budget professional depends on how often you'll use that photo and to what degree it will shape customers' impressions of your business. I do a good deal of public speaking and training, so my photo meant a lot.

CASE STUDY: PHOTOS OF THE BUSINESS OR PRODUCT

If you want a photo of your product, location, or something else that isn't you, you have a few choices. One, of course, is to take the picture yourself. Dan, proprietor of Adam's Retreat, decided to go it alone; the mountainous setting for the retreat was simply too beautiful to ruin, even for the most amateur picture-taker. So he bought a digital camera, took lots of pictures, and downloaded them onto his computer. He put the best ones on his website, and thanks to the wonders of software packages, cut and pasted them into a brochure that went out to other major tourist hot spots.

However, Betty of Betty's Pastries found that her efforts to get images strong enough to impress retailers bombed. She simply could not capture the look she needed to achieve with the camera; each picture resembled something from a Betty Crocker bake-off. That's because there were too many variables she needed to control: lighting, angle, setting—all non-issues for Dan. So she hired a pro and a few hundred dollars later had the pictures she wanted.

Obviously, the choice is yours. But a few reminders: If you do it yourself, get a *good* camera. It will make a huge difference in the result. Think simple, too. If you're an amateur, you don't want countless knobs to turn or dimensions to adjust until you get the right angle. Finally, take lots and lots of shots. Even the most professional photographer takes hundreds, then picks the ones she likes best.

There's also plenty of clip art around. The only problem is that the truly beautiful or other impressive ones are specific to a location or individual. Dan, for example, could have picked from hundreds of mountainous views, but if they happened to be the Himalayas, what good would that do? As for the generic pictures of people sitting around a board-room, forget it. They're about as provocative as . . . well, people sitting around a boardroom.

Bios

You need bios for everything your marketing heart desires. Trust me, sooner or later they'll prove indispensable.

Cost

Almost free, meaning it costs only for your time and any assistance you get.

Use

Bios have various lengths and functions. You need to include them in your brochures, news releases, direct mail pieces, proposals, and the About Us section of your website. They'll convince editors to feature you or your business in their publications as an expert in your field, help businesses decide to hire you and not the other guy, lend credibility to your brochure or newsletter, and encourage visitors to continue touring your site—and hopefully pursue your products and services after they do.

The question arises as to how many bios you actually need. Just you, if you're the owner of the company? How about your key employees? And your business? Do you need a bio for that as well? The answer is "yes" to all the above. Remember, bios are short, the price is right, and it can't hurt to have them. So go ahead.

What to Do

Bios are pretty formulaic, but like anything in marketing, you need to emphasize whatever aspect of your message will most appeal to customers. Basically, bios come in three sizes: the full bio that's roughly one page, and should include your photo; the one-paragraph bio for your brochures, newsletters, and other pieces; and the one-liner that you slip into ads, coupons, and other short pieces. Your tagline may fill this function, depending on how you write it.

Here's what you do:

Step 1. Start by writing a one-page bio about yourself if you are a significant feature of your organization. For example, if you own a restaurant and have Cordon Bleu training, have won awards, and have been featured in culinary magazines, you are your best selling point. If you own a chain of cool 1950s retro diners, the jukeboxes and burgers will be a better marketing hook. Some business owners also include one-pagers about their business, although normally, the less-is-better philosophy reigns. Don't worry about writing a full bio for anyone else! The one-paragraph version will be enough.

This is how your one-pager should look:

Paragraph one: Introduces the most valuable aspects of your professional life—as the customer will perceive them. For example, look at this first paragraph for Suzy Miller, a yoga teacher who also consults on relaxation techniques and has written extensively on the subject.

> Suzy Miller has been helping men and women of all ages find health, peace, and happiness through yoga for almost thirty years. She incorporates the teachings of numerous yoga traditions, including the Anusara style of Hatha yoga. She is certified in Rising Sun Yoga Therapy and by the National Yoga Institute based in Tucson.

Paragraphs two, three, and four: This is where you write other aspects of your professional life that *directly* connect with your business, but are not as important to your customer. Unless you are a recent college grad, put your education last. So here is what Suzy would say:

> She also works in numerous health facilities using yoga as an invaluable path to helping patients recover or end their lives in the

most comfortable way possible. As a consultant, she has trained nurses and other health care providers to mix yoga techniques into Western approaches to medicine, especially when working with severely traumatized and dying patients.

Articles about Suzy's techniques have appeared in *Women's Health and Healing* magazine, *Good Life Times*, and numerous other newspapers and magazines. Suzy also contributes regularly to the online publication *Fitness and Wellness Today*. Her yoga classes have been cited as the Best in California by the Greater California Fitness Association, and speakers including Dr. Melvin Fenty have espoused her professionalism.

A certified nurse, Suzy Miller graduated from the University of Pittsburgh and received her RN from Boston University. She lives in Freemont, California, with her husband and their six cats.

One bio does not fit every demand, and you will have to revise yours depending on who receives it. In the example above, Suzy was writing to prospective participants for her yoga classes. But if she's hoping to consult at hospitals, hospices, and other medical establishments on relaxation techniques for their patients, she'd probably rewrite her first paragraph this way:

Suzy Miller, a registered nurse and certified yoga instructor, has used yoga to help patients transition back into health or through their end-of-life journey. As a consultant, she has trained nurses and other care providers to mix yoga with Western approaches. Articles about Suzy's techniques have appeared in *Women's Health and Healing* magazine, *Good Life Times*, and numerous newspapers and magazines. Suzy also contributes regularly to the online publication *Fitness and Wellness Today*.

Naturally, the question arises about whether you should put personal information in your bio. In Suzy's case, she was trying for the personal touch, giving clients a glimpse of her private life. If you happen to be a pediatrician, an education consultant, a children's book writer, or a nutritionist, go ahead and mention your kids. But if you're a researcher engaged in a project to find a cure for cancer, mentioning your home life won't help.

Step 2. Cut the bio to its most essential points. This will be your one-paragraph bio for those brochures, newsletters, and other pieces we mentioned earlier. Here's what you do.

Start the bio with the most important point for the customer. In Suzy's case, she wants people to sign up for her classes:

> Certified teacher and registered nurse Suzy Miller has been teaching yoga for almost thirty years, incorporating numerous yoga traditions, including the Anusara style of Hatha yoga.

Then, add details in descending order of importance to your customer.

> Her participants include men and women of all ages, as well as patients and those whose lives are ending. Articles about Suzy's techniques have appeared in *Women's Health and Healing* magazine, *Good Life Times*, and numerous other newspapers and magazines. Suzy also contributes regularly to the online publication *Fitness and Wellness Today*. Her yoga classes have been cited as the Best in California by the Greater California Fitness Association.

Use the same strategy for your business or your employees. Simply draft a list of the most to least important qualities—to the customer— fiddle with the sentence structure, add a few transitions, and you're done!

Step 3. Boil down your bio to one line that you can fit into ads, coupons, and other quick copy. You can adjust these depending on who you're going to reach and why. Here's what Suzy might say on one of her coupons:

Enjoy the peace and happiness of yoga with Suzy Miller—certified yoga instructor, registered nurse, and published expert.

Keep It Professional: Delete any unnecessary and highly personal information from your biographical material. Play golf? Unless you own a golf shop or manage a course, no one really cares. Likewise, they don't care if you've been married for thirty years or spend your weekends in Paris. Interesting, but it doesn't make your product better.

The Resume Question

You may be wondering whether you need to develop a resume as well. Depending on the customer and what you do for a living, you may need to add this to your marketing kit. But don't use the resume in your marketing material. The language is the last thing from interesting or exciting and you want to come off as an industry professional, not an employment seeker.

QUICK Tip

Borrow Good Ideas: Look at the additional samples of bios in Appendix B, and cruise the Web. The About Us section is just loaded with samples—some good, some bad. And while you're at it, try looking in the Press Room part of a few websites. At the bottom of the press release, you'll find those one-paragraph bios. If you look at companies in your industry, you'll also get some good ideas about how your competitors position themselves.

Chapter 7

Brochures

As you can probably guess, these are high on your priority list—but not as high as you think.

Cost

Depends. Brochures can be almost free if you do them yourself, or cost thousands of dollars for a lengthy, glossy model. The more you buy, the less expensive each brochure will be—depending on color and paper, they can cost around a dollar apiece, sometimes less. Many business owners sink a good chunk of their marketing budget into producing them. Then these beauties sit in their back office or warehouse, waiting to be discovered.

So be reasonable. How often will you need the brochure? How central a figure will it play in your marketing strategy? Do you want the brochure for a product, service, or class you're conducting that will have a relatively short shelf life? If you have a brochure for your business, what purpose do you want it to serve? Should it provide information about your offering in general or give information people might use immediately? If you're only handing out two or three a month, you might as well print them on a laser printer in your office. If you use them en masse, go to a professional printer.

Use

You can up the value of your brochure considerably by giving it a utilitarian function, as we've been discussing. For example, right now on my fridge I have two brochures attached with magnets. One is for the Chinese restaurant down the street. The cover has the usual contact information. The inside has the menu. Hungry for takeout? Not sure what to have for dinner? Problem solved. Remember the love at fifth sight idea? Because we see that brochure every day, the Chinese restaurant is the first place we think of when we're too tired to cook. Without it, we'd probably go for pizza or other options nearby.

The second brochure is for the Goose Route Dance Company. Two pluses have earned this marketing piece refrigerator status. One is the image on the cover: a dancer striking an elegant pose. This is a nonprofit dance company, and the paper is your basic stock, copied on a home printer. But still, the picture has enough visual appeal to make it worth a daily look. Inside is the class and concert schedule, which serves the same function as the Chinese restaurant's brochure: reminding me that classes are waiting, even on days I feel too tired to go.

Other utilitarian uses for your brochure:
  • Time-sensitive coupons on the back encouraging people to purchase
  • Tips, maps, or other information with refrigerator or bulletin-board appeal, so customers think of you the instant they need your service

• Sample packets of your product if it's food, cosmetics, or another easy-to-package item—while this may be pricey, the sample will tease customers into wanting more and draw an enduring connection between you and them

• Price lists of your product with contact information *immediately* available so they can call you to order what they want, or see if you have their sizes

Naturally, your brochure does need to serve its most common and obvious function: to tell the customer about your offerings. But remember, it's imperative that you keep the biographical information at a minimum and use the reader-focus orientation we discussed in chapter 4.

What to Do

Determine some design features of your brochure. I say "some," because you already know the color and general look from your business cards. These, naturally enough, reflect the brand we reviewed earlier. But do you want a three-fold brochure? A four-color flyer that you fold into a booklet?

Think out of the box, too! And consider these facts about your customers: they don't like to turn pages, they aren't wild about reading, and they want immediate gratification. So maybe you want a postcard-style "brochure" on heavier stock that might look like an enlarged business card. On one side, put your logo, tagline, and other signature information, along with a great visual, and on the other side, four- or five-line paragraphs—perhaps a bulleted list—of your offerings. If you can offer advice or helpful hints, too, all the better.

If you own a bookstore, you probably give away bookmarks at the front counter. Consider these for your brochure. Need to make them bigger? Go ahead. You may want to add a timely quality, too, such as this month's best reads, hits from the *New York Times* bestseller list, or even better, dates of sales at your store to ensure they keep coming in. The possibilities are endless, so don't limit yourself to what everyone else is doing.

Here are some basics about creating your brochure. Stay tuned—you'll find some great ideas about how to get your brochures exposure in the next section.

The Cover: Catch 'Em

Earlier in this book, we discussed the importance of making an intriguing first impression. The cover of your brochure is the place to do it. Here's what it should contain:

• A "hook" of some sort that intrigues and invites your customer. You may achieve this with your tagline. Or perhaps you need to add something a little spicier, such as the question: "Why does your car need Rhone Shine today?" Or a promise to provide information: "Want to avoid rust and corrosion? Look inside to see how." Or another promise of some sort—just be sure to keep it realistic: "Rhone Shine: the treatment that could help you avoid thousands of dollars of damage to your car."

• Your name, address, phone number, and email address

• Your web address positioned so the customer can easily see it

• Your logo and tagline

You may want a photo on the cover as well. Photos are great and can help your brochure compete with all the other messages thrown at your customer. Just make sure it's consistent with your brand and intriguing to the customer.

Inner columns: Quick and Clean

The key to a great brochure can be summed up in one word: underload. No, you don't want to overload your customer with word use. But don't even give them the same amount as, say, a direct mail piece. Give them less. Instead, think length (short, as in four- or five-line paragraphs, and not a lot of them) and variety (bulleted lists are great, but so are call-outs and testimonials).

Here are some options for your brochure—and just about every other marketing message!

1. Testimonials

You see these all the time on television, and they work wonders. You know—a slender, beautiful woman tells you how she lost forty-five pounds in only three weeks. Or a calm, smiling homemaker shows you her son's shirt before and after that All NEW! detergent worked its wonders.

Here's why: if you claim your business brings outstanding results, who will believe you? And why should they? What else are you going to say? But when someone says it for you, that's different.

Your testimonials can be compliments: "I never expected Rhone Shine to be so easy to use!" or anecdotes: "I noticed the rust on my car. My mechanic recommended Rhone Shine. I'd seen my neighbor using it, so I figured, why not? My car never looked so good." Either way, be specific when possible: "Nineteen dollars a bottle is much better than the thousands of dollars I probably would have spent for repairs."

2. Myths and realities/true and false statements

You can grab the customers' attention on the front of your brochure and keep it throughout with these little marketing devices:

Myth and reality: These are prevailing myths your customer has certainly heard. Make the myths true *myths*, not just false information. Here's an example:

Myth: On full moons, emergency rooms have more patients, fire departments are busier, and mental hospitals have more admissions.

Reality: Thirty-six studies concur: the full moon does not change the rate of emergencies or even individual behavior.

True and false: Just what it says. Only the information must make the customer think.

True or false: During a full moon, more people get into car accidents, end up in emergency rooms, or are admitted to mental hospitals.

3. Questions and answers

These are by far the most used, overused, and underestimated devices around. Essentially, when good, they beg for answers. To make them work, though, remember these Q&A rules:

• Make them sound interesting. ("What is the leading cause of corrosion on cars today?" and not "What is the leading cause of the corrosive effects due to environmental factors on your automobile?")

• Include information the reader can use. ("Sure, corrosion seems inevitable, but you can take steps to stop it.")

• Give a detailed answer, not a "yes" or "no."

4. Direct action

Tell your customers to do something when reading your message. Make it fun, make it interesting, and make it matter! For example, give them a checklist of safety features they should have around their house. As they check, comment on their responses. Do they have a smoke alarm? Remind them to clean it and change the batteries. If they check no, tell them to get one.

Or tell them to get a pencil and paper, then have them do some sort of calculation on the page. It's critical that this exercise bring some interesting and usable result. This will create a truly interactive engagement; you and the reader have worked together on a complete project.

Back Column: Bio, Tips, Coupons

Remember that one-paragraph bio you wrote? This is the place to put it. If you didn't have a tip sheet, think about putting one here. Or put your customer's address here and send the brochure as a mailer.

QUICK Tip

Use Good Paper: You'll have lots of options when it comes to paper, but a word of caution: stay away from the flimsier varieties—they droop—and go for the sturdier stock.

What's Next . . .

Once you have finished your brochure, here are some great ideas about how to make it work for you:

• Put it on the Web. You may want to upload it as is, or scatter pieces of it around the site. For example, your bio would go under About Us and your list of services would go under Services.

Use a brochure distribution service. These guys take your brochures and distribute them basically everywhere. According to CTM Brochure Display, which caters to tourist and visitor destinations, they can help you reach twelve million customers. Basically you buy a package based on target audience, geographic location, and demographics. The distribution costs vary—approximately five to ten dollars a month for each location. The customers are generally prequalified; they take the brochures because they want to.

• Leave it in places your customer is bound to go. Remember Dan, the owner of Adam's retreat? He leaves his brochures all over the place: in local shops and restaurants catering to tourists, and laundromats where tourists, often staying in rustic cabins, wash their clothes. Either way, he talks to the proprietor to get her permission, strikes up a relationship, and gets her to recommend his retreat should anyone ask.

• By the way, Dan also leaves his brochure in several of the local real estate offices, too. Tourists continually stroll in asking if the proprietors know any cabins they could rent for a week or two. Naturally, the proprietor gives them the Adam's Retreat brochure. In exchange, Dan gives the realtors 20 percent off his cabin rental fee.

QUICK Tip

Find the Best: There's an association for brochure distribution services, aptly named the International Association of Brochure Distributors (www.APBD.org). Even if you're not planning to distribute your brochures beyond your local community, this site is definitely worth a virtual visit. It contains lots more information about composing a brochure and even hosts a fabulous brochure award. Thumb through their archives to get ideas from the very best!

• Bring it to conferences—but don't bring it alone! Everyone and their brother-in-law will be passing out brochures. So attach a tip sheet, special offer, giveaway if it's small, or anything else that sets your brochure apart. And if possible, partner with booths in complementary fields—they'll display your brochure (or at least your business card) and you'll display theirs.

Alert!

Making Multiple Brochures: You may want to create lots of brochures: one that provides information about your company, one that's great for a special offer at a conference, and one that announces a new product. Here are few reminders for all of them:

• Think response! We talked about the response mechanism earlier. Make sure each brochure targets a direct response from your customer that's action-oriented! Avoid thinking you want them to remember you, like you, understand your product, or enjoy your brochure. Focus on what you want them to do: call you, save your brochure, buy your product, pass your brochure on to someone else, file it in their office for future reference, and check your website for more details.

• Use your previous brochure template, or something close to it, for all your new ones. This means you can reproduce them faster, for less expense, and have that all-important brand consistency we talked about earlier. And you can keep certain parts, like your bio, in the new version.

CASE STUDY: CHECK ORIGINALITY

Betsy Mendelssohn wanted a great brochure to publicize her spa, but didn't have the funds to do it. So she purchased a packet, got some great clip art off the Web, and scanned some photos of the place. She brought the brochures to a professional women's group meeting and put them on the table highlighting members' companies. As she collected the remaining few when leaving, guess what she saw a few brochures down? One using the exact same template for a family construction company.

Need some inspiration? Turn to Appendix B for another brochure example.

Chapter 8

Almost Everything You Need to Know about Creating Your Website

Read this section whether you have a website or not. It will contain lots of ideas you can add in!

Cost

That's up to you. You can get a web design kit at your local office supply store for as low as fifty dollars. Or you can hire a website designer. Their prices can range from five hundred dollars (especially if they're just getting started) to thousands of dollars. Websites can also have hidden costs, depending on the versatility of your site, how you market it, and how often you or someone else updates it. And while the Web can be a great moneymaker, it's a prime example of having to market your marketing. But don't worry: at the end of this chapter we'll discuss ways you can market your website for almost free.

Use

The Web is so diverse, it's almost breathtaking. Many small businesses ignore or forgo websites, especially food establishments or retail operations, and why should they have one? Their customer is right there, walking through the door. My advice in that case: don't do it!

The Web can, however, open countless possibilities. Here are a few:

• **New avenues for selling your product or service**. The beauty of the virtual visitor is that he's there because he wants to be, as opposed to the real-life visitor who might just be walking past your door. Granted, some are casual observers or competitors, but odds are you'll mostly get visitors with a heightened interest in what you're selling, and a heightened likelihood they'll buy.

• **New avenues for diversifying your offering**. Let's say you're a corporate trainer. Think of all the training material you've compiled over the years! Why not collect it, bind it, and sell it over the Web as a workbook. If you own a bookstore—especially a specialty or antique bookstore—perhaps compile a list of valuable books that you know are hard (or easy) to find and sell the list online. The possibilities can go on and on, no matter what you do for a living. And the beauty is you don't have to stretch your offerings. Just focus on what you already have!

• **Greater personal presence**. Don't limit yourself to print and still-life photos. You can add videos, voiceovers, just about anything you want to your site to have the greatest effect. Oh, and since people from San Francisco to Shanghai might view it, be careful of using regionalisms or local references.

• **Countless networking opportunities**. I'm speaking, of course, about links, those wonderful virtual partnerships. Of course, you'll need to find websites that will link yours to theirs, but unlike traditional networking, you can do it without leaving your desk. More on this later.

Grab Their Attention: Your reader reacts to your message in fifty milliseconds. And with the "halo effect," that's a reaction that keeps on giving—or not, depending on how well you manage your message.

What to Do

Step 1: Design Your Website

The least expensive and possibly fastest way of getting started is to get a website package at your local office supply store. Or you can hire a pro who knows about the nuances of web appeal. If you do, be sure you can get into your website yourself to make regular updates, additions, and other changes. It's amazingly easy to do and will keep your site fresh. Or you can do both. Hire a pro to help you get your website up and advise you on ways to polish and finish it. My advice: don't go it alone. The Web is simply too important to your marketing strategy to waste all that virtual space it occupies.

Step 2: Pick a Name

Everything we said about names is true. They reflect your brand. They must sound interesting yet familiar. And with websites, they must be easy for your customer to guess. In the perfect world, you'd simply write your business name and throw a ".com" at the end. But this is an imperfect—and overpopulated—world, so you may have to tweak a little.

I wanted my website, for example, to be susanbenjamin.com. Easy enough—except another Susan Benjamin has it. Never mind that she's in England and isn't a writer. It's hers. So, I had to use susanfbenjamin.com, using my middle initial to make the distinction. Sounds easy, right? Actually, no. I now have to use "Susan F. Benjamin" in everything I produce, from books to lighthearted emails. But getting people to my site is that important.

Step 3: Add Content

Here's what you need to know about presenting your information:

• Think hook. Your home page is everything—and it's critical that you instantly hook visitors. Don't rule out Q&As, the promise of freebies, or interesting tips. Own an oil company? "Want a list of the Ten Best Ways to Save Fuel this season? Click here!" would work nicely. Then, have them email their request. Be sure to send them a list immediately. And add their email address to your prospect list.

• Find easy-to-purchase methods for every page. Make your product or service immediately available with toll-free numbers and links to your company's email address on just about every page. And don't forget to give visitors the option to pay online with a credit card, sign up for a session, or apply for any club membership you might offer. Don't have a company club? Think about it. Your local supermarket does, with those discount cards. So why not you?

• Use interesting visuals. Ever hear the expression "eye candy"? Well, put some on every page. Photographs are great, but any other eye-catching, brand-matching images will work, too.

• Use strategies of engagement to turn an altogether passive visitor into an active participant in your message. The most common, and fun for your visitor, are tests. If you read magazines, you've probably taken multiple-choice tests countless times with promises of incredible insights at the end, like "Take Your Love Life I.Q." or "Are You Eating the Right Food for Your Lifestyle?"

Obviously, you don't have to write about love or food to use multiple-choice questions. Make sure your quiz is informative, fascinating, and engaging, and that the answers reveal why the visitors need you and which of your services are perfect for them.

Here are some tricks to remember, if you go this interesting route:

Trick 1: Give them a good reason to take the test.

Trick 2: Make sure each item contains usable information. If you're talking about safety features in their house, don't state obvious information like telling them gas leaks are bad.

Trick 3: Make the information interesting. Stats are always good, so you could give them the following multiple-choice quiz:

Eighty-five percent of all fires occur in:

A. Forests

B. Homes

C. Work sites

D. Highway accidents

The answer, in case you didn't know, is homes. Regardless, stay away from obvious or flat-sounding information.

Multiple-choice tests aren't the only ones around. Try I.Q. tests, as in: "Learn Your Safety I.Q." Or rate their knowledge about financial issues or road safety. They can click on a different page for an answer or a catchy analysis of what the results mean.

• Last and not at all least, make sure you have each of those Ten Marketing Imperatives from the first part of this section *nailed*.

Step 4: Update Your Site

Do this regularly. A good site is a fresh site the visitor will return to again and again. And don't forget the marketing opportunities, such as offering a "Web only" deal where you might promise your customers a discount if they print out coupons from your site. This will get them to learn more about you, let them see your other offerings, and, hopefully, give them reasons to return again, especially if you hook them with promises like "Check our weekly [or monthly] coupons here!"

Step 5: Check Results

Who's visiting your site? Where are they going when they do? You can find out and market and change accordingly.

Market Your Marketing

You can take numerous steps to entice people to visit your site. Here are some of them:

• **Put your website address on *everything* you produce.** That means tips sheets, ads, flyers, and your email signature block. Put it in your shop window, if you have one, on your brochures, and on every give-away from the thinnest pens to the brightest Frisbees.

• **Invest in search advertising.** This feature is free up to a point. You know how when you search for products or services, a bar with the addresses of businesses that supply or otherwise address whatever item you're searching for appears? Well, the description is free and attracts the attention of millions of potential visitors. However, once they click through, you must pay ten to fifteen cents for every click you get.

• **Link, link, link.** Think complementary. In other words, a company links to your website and you link to theirs. Here are a few places to consider:

> Associations with an interest in what you do
> Associations in which you're a member
> State, local, and federal agencies who link consumers to businesses that provide specific services
> Businesses who offer a related service
> Businesses whose lines you carry in your store
> Businesses with whom you have relations
> Online publications who may have quoted you and who have a resource list for their readers

• **Position yourself on a search engine.** You probably use search engines dozens of times a day at least. Certainly, the names of the search engines are familiar: Google, Yahoo, and plenty of others. The trick to search engines is how the customer gets to *your* site and not those gazillions of other possible sites that show up when they search.

So, here's what you do. Narrow down your offering to a few key words. If you offer flight lessons, you'd list "flight lessons" (no surprise), and possibly a few details like "stunt flying" or the kinds of airplanes you fly. If you're in import-export, you may have to narrow down considerably to your primary product and trade location. Then, submit your site to the search engines, being sure to mention those words as many times as possible throughout your site. Obviously, be as natural about it as possible.

• Keep track. If you're not getting the volume you want or can reasonably expect, go back and make adjustments. Get the baseline information from your host provider—find out which pages are most popular, which search words customers use, when they go in and out, and which pages they access while they're there.

By the way, you can up your link-potential significantly by offering tips and other information your visitors can use for their own sakes. Accentuate these offerings on the home page. Oh, and keep it real: don't use the pretense of advice to mask a sales pitch.

QUICK Tip

Search Engine Strategies: There are plenty of free or almost-free options for getting exposure on the Web. Some search engines, such as Google, cost nothing to get on. To submit your site, go to http://www.google.com/addurl/?continue=/addurl. Then when a customer uses their search engine, your site appears.

Also try DMOZ.org, which lets you hit lots of search engines at one time. The trick, as always, is targeting the right words. Then, look at the data your website host provides you, also for free, and decide whether and how you want to get into one of the pay search engines such as Yahoo and MSN.
—Johnna Armstrong, www.biztechsource.com

QUICK Tip

Find What Works: Spend time traveling in the virtual world. You probably do this already to get directions, to buy tickets, and for countless other reasons. But this is different. Visit sites for the sole purpose of looking and learning. See what other businesses are doing. Borrow some ideas. Try to identify mistakes. If the site doesn't seem quite good enough, make sure your site isn't doing the same. Perhaps you want to keep a small notebook of website ideas. Don't have time? Have an employee do it for you.

QUICK Tip

Explore Other Online Options: You have an increasing number of options to make an online presence—far too many to detail here. But here's a list you may want to investigate further:

- Discussion boards

- Blogs

- Newsgroups

- Electronic newsletters

- Chat rooms

Obviously, these options aren't right for everyone, and before committing yourself to any of them, determine whether your primary client uses them, whether you have the time to keep up with them, whether your offering lends itself to this kind of presence (a lobbying firm, yes; a septic system cleaner, no), and whether you're comfortable with the written form.

Chapter 9

Direct Mail and Email Marketing

Direct Mail Pieces

Direct mail pieces—to do or not to do? The answer: depends. Think your options through carefully before investing in this marketing uncertainty, and keep track of the response, in terms of dollars, that you get.

Cost

Printer ink and paper, labor, and postage. If you want to buy mailing lists, factor these in, too. They can range from one hundred to five hundred dollars and usually are good for one mailing. By the way, you can use an auto-responder—a service that instantly delivers your info to potential customers. These guys do everything but supply the list—a definite "no" in the antispam world of email marketing, and a good idea for all businesses to follow.

You supply the content and they'll send your customer your direct mail, or other marketing piece, in whatever sequence you determine. For example, say your customer signs up on your website (auto-responders also provide the web forms) for a research document you just produced. The auto-responder will send that, with a follow-up letter, the day after. Then, a week or two later, they'll send your newsletter, and whatever else you like. The auto-responder also sends broadcasts of everything from grand openings at your field offices to upcoming seminars and guest appearances.

All this, according to an associate at Pennsylvania-based Aweber Communications, for a mere $19.95 a month. The price includes storing ten thousand subscribers—add another $9.95 for your next ten thousand. Still, that's pretty almost-free!

Use

Direct mail pieces are the most controversial of the marketing piece clan. Some people open them to see what's inside, while others toss them with barely a nod to the envelope. Another name for direct mail, as I'm sure you know, is "junk mail."

So, what is the difference between an effective marketing piece and junk?

The answer has nothing to do with the piece at all. It's your recipient. Send your direct mail to the general world, and forget it. But send it to the right customer, and it can do wonders. Here are a few possible uses:

• **Announcements.** Announcements can be great because they naturally have an exciting quality. But make sure that your customer has a reason to care. Sure, you can announce a new partner. This keeps customers abreast of changes in your firm, but it does something even better. It touches on their sense of "exclusivity," making them feel like one of the crowd. If they read about the arrangement later in the business section of the paper, all the better—they heard it first!

• **Invitations.** These are wonderful ways of tapping into the customer's sense of exclusivity. The invitation, whether to your open house, exhibit, talk, or other event, really isn't open to the public—just those lucky enough to get an invite. Just make sure they know from the envelope that an invitation is enclosed, and what they'll get when they arrive. By the way, make sure plenty of friends and associates will be there when the customer arrives, just in case you have a thin turnout.

• **Samples, coupons, and other giveaways.** If you have any that are easy to package and cheap to send, why not? Or send time-sensitive coupons. They'll appreciate the gesture and have a reason to come. How about bookmarks, if you happen to be in publishing, training, or some other bookish profession? Newsletters are also great, especially one-pagers, although most people probably prefer receiving these online—definitely a cheaper option.

• **A product offer.** Give some urgency to the way you word the mailing. We talked about this earlier—the short sentences. The excited, almost breathless rhythm of the piece. The direct mail piece will encourage customers to call or email you for more information. Then, hopefully, they'll buy. Or you can include a postage-paid business response card they can use when they immediately fall in love with your product and order it on the spot.

In terms of effectiveness, the numbers vary. Some say you should expect a 10 percent response rate, others a 50 percent response rate, depending on who and how well you're targeting. According to marketing consultant Chris Cardell, you should test, test, test. Get a good response? Send your direct mail pieces out a few weeks later and plan on getting another good response—about half of the first mailing.

By the way, he also recommends adhering to the break-even concept. If you break even on your mailing, consider it a success. Some of those customers are bound to bring in repeat business—and the profits will begin.

What to Do

Naturally, before you have a direct mail campaign, you need a list. And lists there are aplenty. You can get list of everyone by age, gender, location, buying habits, you name it. But don't forget, you have to pay for these lists and the response is uncertain.

So, here are two pointers that should help: if you do buy lists, try to narrow them down to your primary customer, the one you identified at the beginning of this book. Second, whenever possible, add or focus exclusively on customers you have identified directly by a guestbook in your shop, an email you may have received, or a referral.

Next, think strategy. Remember those Ten Imperatives of Marketing Material? Well, you must adhere to every one—on the envelope of your direct mail piece, first, then in the real thing. In fact, if you can get the customer to open your direct mail piece you have, as they say, won half the battle.

So what's a businessperson to do? As always, be imaginative and let the thoughts and ideas flow directly from your instinct and the culture of your business. Given that, here are some possibilities:

State the offer up front. Promising them 25 percent off? Important Information that Could Change Your Life?! Limit yourself to a short sentence, using natural-sounding language—none of the "Enclosed within" or "Exclusive management software tools inside" type of talk. And no jargon, please!

State the purpose of the direct mail piece. If you're sending your customer discount coupons, an invitation, or a sample, let them know on the envelope. "An Exclusive Invitation," "Coupons Inside," and "Tell us what you think!" all work well.

Use humor. Anything (tasteful) goes here. How about a riddle? Or a lightbulb joke? If you're sending members of the American Psychiatric

Association a subscription to your newsletter, how about writing, "How many psychiatrists does it take to change a lightbulb?" on the outside. Then, the moment they open the direct mail piece, they'll see the answer: "One, but the lightbulb must want to change." Then, add something like: " . . . and you'll get all the information you need about lightbulbs and more serious matters in the psychiatric field by top researchers such as Dr. Edward Johansson and Carolyn Shaffer, MD, PhD, in *Psychologist Newsletter.*"

Make a promise. These can be as a flip or as serious as you want. For example, the newsletter could say: "We have something that could revolutionize your practice." Or if you own a photography studio, how about "Photo of Elvis Inside"? When they open the envelope, there's Elvis and a coupon for 10 percent off all holiday photos of the kids in the first two weeks of November.

Of course, another option is to skip the envelope altogether and send a postcard. The price is cheap: for 750 cards plus stamps, you pay only about $300, depending on paper and copy requirements. You don't have to fold your direct mail piece or hire someone to do it, and even better, the customer will immediately see your offer whether they want to or not. Remember to keep the visuals flashy and that a few words work wonders. So avoid: "You can save 25% or more, depending on your purchase, May 15–20" and go for "Save 25% PLUS, May 15–20."

As for the body of your direct mail piece, tradition has it that you should send a letter. But tradition is fast fading as more and more customers refuse to read direct mail pieces. Think about it: do you? I don't. I'm just too busy. But I will look at a bright flyer tucked into the envelope or use a pen, bookmark, or other interesting freebie attached to a brief note.

But if you must use direct mail letters, here are some dos and don'ts:

Do: Get to the point—your offer or other pitch—of your direct mail piece in the first line or two of your letter.

Don't: Drag the opening on with boring information or goofy questions like: "Do you want to save money on your heating bills?" Never give them obvious information such as "The cost of heating has skyrocketed" or start with phrases such as "As you probably know . . ." or "In the event that. . . ."

Do: Follow your first paragraph with a paragraph or two of support material, such as details of your offering or testimonials. Close by telling them other ways to reach you.

Don't: Enter points randomly. Make sure you have a clear order of information, moving from the most to the least compelling point— although they should *all* be compelling in one way or another. By the way, beware of the two gravest problems direct mail writers confront: repeating the point of your first paragraph in your second, or worse, throughout the letter, and burying the most important point in the last or second-to-last paragraph.

Do: Limit your paragraphs to five lines or so—and use bullets. White space is key to the visibility of your message.

Don't: Have long, burdensome paragraphs or let your letter meander into a second page.

Do: Include testimonials.

Don't: Brag.

And *definitely* **do** adhere to the Ten Marketing Imperatives. Be sure to use the checklist when you're done.

Want to see a sample? Go to Appendix B.

QUICK Tip

Almost-Free Direct Mail Pieces: Here's what you do. Get together with one, two, even three other businesses with complementary offerings. Then decide on a sale or some other strategy that will create a focus for the direct mail piece. Design it yourself, on a postcard, and combine lists. You've probably tripled the numbers of customers you'll reach and shrunk the cost. Remember we said around seven hundred postcards should cost about $300 all told. Cut that in half, then thirds . . . You reach your customers and plenty of others for far less money (and effort) than if you did it yourself.

Alert!

Always, Always, Always: Include your web address where the customer can immediately see it!

Money marketing rule

Don't make your customers work! Do the work for them. That means sending along self-addressed stamped envelopes or return postcards where appropriate. Have an envelope? Make sure it's easy to open. Some people like to send FedExes, too. If you go bulk, you can probably get away with six dollars apiece. That's a lot compared to the price of your average stamp, but it will most likely get their attention. But don't make them sign for it. And if you decide to go postal, make sure mail carriers will deliver your message with their usual load—don't make your customer take an extra trip to the post office to pick it up.

Direct Emails

These have the same risks as direct mail pieces and the same rewards.

Cost

Labor, lists, and the cost of an online distributor, if you use one. Of course, you could just stick to the almost-free option and use lists you collect yourself. By automating your email functions, you'll cut the expense of your time even further.

Use

Emails are a great way to get visibility for your business—even if customers don't open them. Only a few caveats here. You may know them already, but don't let them slip under your radar.

The line between an emailed direct mail piece and spam can be thin—as in thin as ice. So you need to reach preapproved customers—preapproved by themselves, that is, by at least one of the ways we already discussed in the earlier part of this chapter, such as having them fill in your guestbook.

And thanks to the wonders of the vast e-world, they can respond to your offer simply by clicking. You can also set up e-clubs where customers get special buys unavailable anywhere else. The tourist and airline industries use these a lot. Certainly, for most offerings, you can too.

What to Do

Email your customer every month with a new offer, but be careful. Too much (more than once a month) and you're a nuisance; not enough (less than once a month) and they forget you. Or you can send them regular tip sheets—or even better, a newsletter—chock-full of interesting and timely information. You can advertise for your free newsletter in e-magazines and the paper editions. Plaster your newsletter with your website address and store your customers' addresses for other direct email pieces you send.

Here are some other pointers:

Have an interesting—make that riveting—subject line. Treat the subject line as the hook you put on your envelope when mailing a hard copy. Keep it tight—maybe four or five words—and use plenty of verbs. Notice the difference here:

No verbs: An invitation

Verbs: Please come, May 16

No verbs: Fanny's Flowers

Verbs: Remember Fanny on Feb 14

No verbs: Newsletter

Verbs: New depression findings from *Psychology Newsletter*

Notice on the last sample I wrote *Psychology Newsletter* in the subject line. Always be careful of your content sounding even remotely spam-like, and let the customer know your identity. True, they can see it in the "from" column, but be abundantly clear about your legitimacy.

Limit your email to one or two paragraphs. Unless you're sending a newsletter, keep it short, as in one or two paragraphs. And nowhere is the concise word use we discussed in the Ten Imperatives section of this book quite so important. One unnecessary word and you've lost them. And reader-focused? Amazing!

Avoid attachments, if possible. Make the email easy. Even if you have an e-newsletter, keep all the text right there in the email, with links if customers want to learn more. Chances are, they won't open the attachment and may even dismiss your email altogether.

For examples of direct email pieces, see Appendix B.

QUICK Tip

Experiment! Experiment, especially if you're torn about which e-approach works best. Here's what you do: decide on a target group of twenty primary customers. Be particular: all must have some key characteristics in common. They may be women in their mid-thirties with kids and disposable income. Or you may want working professionals in the greater Boston area. Divide the group in two. Label one Group A and the other Group B, or whatever label you like. Then send each group a separate version of your direct mail or email piece and test the response. If possible, expand the test and send to one hundred customers. You should learn something conclusive about what works best.

Chapter 10

Short Stash: Tip Sheets and Flyers

Tip Sheets

Rank tip sheets high on your priority list. Trust me. They're the ultimate in free (if you place them on your website) and almost free (if you print and/or mail them) marketing.

Tips are every business owner's ticket to maximizing exposure by providing something valuable for the customer and positioning themselves as the expert. Even better, they're remarkably easy to write, requiring nothing more than a cool lead paragraph and lots of steps or bullets. And they're the most versatile and useful little marketing creations around—they need only be three or four points, or could go to a full page with five points followed by paragraphs that provide detail. I'm just stunned more businesspeople don't use them.

Like a great ad, tips can accentuate the customer's need for your offering. For example, say you own an automotive repair shop. The tips will tell customers how to check for potential problems. Obviously, one of the steps will be regular tune-ups and oil changes—and they'll know where to go. Just make sure your tips contain information the customer really needs, and not simply those bits that serve your interests.

Tip sheets also highlight your professionalism without you having to state it. No, you don't have to claim you and your team are the best mechanics in the business. You prove it in the tips. Even better, tips are prescriptive: they're the how-to style that flies off of bookstore shelves and blankets the pages of most magazines. In other words, your customer loves to read them!

Just as good, tips create a bond between you and the customer. You give customers something that makes their lives better, and they'll appreciate you for it. Then there's the refrigerator appeal I mentioned earlier in this book. Give them the right tips, and the tips will appear—with your name, number, and web address at the bottom of the page—on the refrigerator, bulletin board, and countless other places.

You can create an independent tip sheet or drop a series of tips into all sorts of marketing materials. Here are just a few:

• **Business cards.** Put your tips on the back—no lead line or paragraph necessary here! A few words only.

• **Brochures**. Tips fit nicely in a small column on one part of the brochure, or they can occupy an entire back page with a perforation so the customer can cut and save. Breaks the cycle of boasting nicely.

• **Newsletter articles.** People love to see tips in magazines and newspapers, so why not in your newsletter? You can write an entire article based on tips. Or use them as a sidebar—that shaded or otherwise offset area that supports the main article.

• **Calendars.** Depends on the calendar. You can have tips in the margin, directly on key days of the month, or have a tip of the month.

• **Direct mail pieces.** Include the tips with your direct mail piece, but dress them up a little. Have a little money to spare? Laminate them. Put them on a magnet with your web address and logo discreetly at the bottom or top. Or print them on a good hearty stock and include vital information that the customer will feel compelled to post somewhere.

• **Websites.** Put them everywhere. A tip of the week on your home page. A tip page that you change regularly. Or insert them in your offerings pages as a column in the margins.

• **News releases.** We'll talk about news releases in greater detail later. For now, though, suffice it to say that your news release could actually *be* a tip sheet. Editors love it, because they can provide valuable and usable information to their readers, and you'll get the exposure you crave. Only one caveat: the tips must be new; provide information you learned through a unique experience, research, or a related task; and provide information the publication's readers can use *immediately*.

• **Conferences, seminars, and other training programs.** Sure, tip sheets are great if you're giving the talk. But spread them around wherever possible even if you aren't. Plenty of conferences have a brochure table for their attendees, so put them there. Obviously, if you have your own booth, display them there, too.

What to Do

As I said, tip sheets are easy. Have an interesting opening, alerting the reader to why this tip sheet is valuable. Make sure the customer feels a clear sense of urgency. Notice the difference in wording and the elicited response:

Ho-hum: "There are lots of ways individuals can limit the cost of repairs to their cars. In fact, breakdowns and related problems can total thousands of dollars each year."

Motivating: "You could be wasting thousands of dollars each year on repairs to your car. But you can lower or even eliminate those expenses. Here are five things you should do."

QUICK Tip

Use a Number: Notice that the sample contained five things the customer can do. Numbering your tips, or just about anything else you want someone to do, can be helpful. The customer knows the list has a starting and ending point, which encourages her to use it. Also, you up the chance she'll keep reading even if she finds one item on the list irrelevant or boring.

Generally, go for round numbers, like ten, twenty, fifty, one hundred, or one thousand, although numbers like fifteen or twenty-five work, too. If you want to go small, try three, five, or seven. No fours, eights, or nines, no matter what you do. Why these numbers work is anyone's guess. But ask yourself how often you see titles like:

The Eight Secrets of Highly Successful People

The Top Nine Most Effective Greetings

Ninety-Seven Steps You Can Take to Improve Your Home

Sound strange, don't they? But what if you only have nine points? Or twenty-three? Do what the experts do: find another one and throw it in. If you're really stretched, weed out the lesser tips, and leave the appropriate number of strong ones.

From there, the body's a snap. Just bullet each item and speak directly to your readers. You can use the "you," as we discussed in Marketing Imperative 3, or speak directly to them in the imperative. So, a typical list for the automotive repair shop chain might read:

To avoid costly repairs take these steps:

• Change your oil regularly.

• Leave your car in a protected environment, especially if you live in a snowy region where the city salts the streets.

• Change your windshield wipers every spring.

You don't have to use bullets, of course. Numbered steps (as in Step 1, Step 2, and Step 3) work well, as do little check marks or little boxes so they can check when each item on the list is complete. Feeling adventurous? Then try using the grandfather of them all: the Q&A. They're great for brochures, articles, and places where you can have lots of copy. Before you do, though, make sure your questions follow these guidelines:

Your questions should:

• **Sound like someone actually said them.** You want your customers to relate to the question as if it just flowed from their own heads. So think authentic. Say you're a tax specialist. The customer probably doesn't sit around thinking, *Hmm, I wonder if there's a way to file my taxes 24/7?* And lay off the jargon. Does anyone actually say, "I wonder if there's a tax plan that will help fortify my assets?" Doubt it.

• **Contain information.** Watch for fluff questions, so insubstantial they practically float away. This is the standard: "Do you want to save money?" This is totally ineffectual—who doesn't? Better to say: "What is the best way to save hundreds—even thousands—of dollars on your taxes? If you don't know the answer, keep reading . . ."

• **Pique the reader's interest.** The questions must deserve—not simply *get*—an answer. If you're writing a tip sheet for a parents' group, you could say, "What is the best proven deterrent for keeping children from taking drugs?" Their minds flit from possibility to possibility: After-school programs? Good friends? A religious affiliation? They look at the answer on the next line or next page and see: "You are."

• **Not require a "yes" or "no" answer.** Take this question: "Do you know the five steps required to ensure your child is safe while riding in your car?" What if the answer is "no"? Okay, they don't know. Now what? Even worse, what if the answer is "yes"? Try sentences that open with "what," "how," and "when," like: "How many steps should you take when getting your child in the car? Two? Three? The answer is five. Here's what they are . . ."

> ## QUICK Tip
>
> Explore the Options: Take out a stack of magazines lying around the house and flip through with an eye for the many different ways they use tips. This should tip *you* off to the many possibilities available for your marketing piece.

Flyers

Unless this is your main source of marketing, like if you have a baby-sitting service or other community-based operation, use these to support your other efforts, but not as a primary tool.

Cost

Your time for developing. If you go to a printer, you pay about forty-eight cents each if you go highbrow for a four-color, single-sided flyer. The price drops to thirty-six cents if you go for fifteen hundred. You can get the price lower than that if you use postcards, print yourself, or lots of other options.

Use

Flyers, as you probably know, are a quick, inexpensive way of getting the word out about an event, from a guest speaker to your business' opening, a sale, or virtually any other matter. On the plus side, they are easy to create, are easy to generate, can easily become a mailer with a quick series of folds, and have outstanding bulletin-board potential at your local grocery store, library, or hardware store. In fact, these babies fit under windshield wipers; in the fold between house and screen doors; on the ledges of restaurants, cafes, and pubs; and countless other places. All for the price of legwork.

On the minus side, think tacky. Flyers just don't have the professional edge of brochures or other marketing pieces. This is partly because they have high dirt potential. Think about the last time you walked down a busy city street and some guy jumped out and handed you a flyer for a local sale. If you took it, you probably dropped it in the trash soon after. Did you happen to notice all the stray flyers around the trash can? In the gutter? On the sidewalk?

Or if you've looked at bulletin boards, did you notice all those little pushpin marks at the top as the flyer gets pushed around from place to place fighting for exposure? As for flyers under windshields—one good rain and you've got colorful mush. Well, you get the picture.

What to Do

The real hook to a successful flyer lies in the visuals. Your flyer should have an interesting and immediate draw for the customer: a photo, words such as sale, or other interesting draws. Make sure your flyer is consistent with your brand. If you reflect an upscale image, keep it upscale. Have photos? Put money into a nice laser reproduction and avoid the hazy image.

Getting the flyers out can be as simple as walking around your community and posting them, hiring someone to hand them out on street corners or otherwise distribute them, or hiring a distribution service. Here are a few more tips:

• **Put them up? Take them down.** Old, curled flyers are a definite disadvantage to your marketing efforts. Some places ask you to date your flyer and they will take them down after a few days or weeks. Other places don't, so check.

• **As-you-go clean-ups.** If you hire people to distribute flyers outdoors, whether handing them to people or placing them on cars, make sure they simultaneously pick up any stray flyers. Oh, and if it rains, even drizzles, they should remove them from car windshields. It's just not fair to leave soggy paper clinging to the windshield for someone else to clean up.

• **Be date-conscious.** Make your offer on the flyer immediate. Announcing a movie for your film festival? Make sure it happens that day or the day after. Then collect the remains and throw them away.

CASE STUDY: AND THE FIRST PRIZE GOES TO . . .

This flyer stood out among a collection of brochures on the ledge of a local candy shop. It consisted of a half-page of nice, thick paper, with some eye-catching pieces of ribbon and yarn of different colors and textures tied through a hole at the edge. On it was typed:

BEGINNING KNITTING LESSONS

Learn basic stitches and how to read a pattern while completing a sampler scarf. All supplies included. Four sessions: Thursday 12–2 p.m. or Saturday 12–2 p.m. $50

River Ridge Fiber Works

(304) 274-9190

If you're male, an engineer, or otherwise can't tell a knitting needle from a chopstick, the brochure would have no appeal. But for anyone with an eye for design, the ribbon alone draws them to the message.

CASE STUDY: AND THE SECOND PRIZE GOES TO . . .

This one is a fabulous idea if you have the funding to do it. Make your flyer so good, so beautiful, your customer will want to save or even frame it. I'm thinking now of the National Geographic movie *March of the Penguins*. The flyer announcing the movie was a definite keep, featuring an adult penguin looking down at its baby. Beautiful! My nine-year-old son hung it in his room, and other people actually framed it and hung it in their houses. The image guaranteed a great showing and stayed on as a reminder when the video came out!

CASE STUDY: AND THE SURPRISE FLYER OF THE YEAR GOES TO . . .

Lest you think flyers work only for homegrown operations: I was walking through Government Center in Boston years ago, when I was approached by a young man passing out flyers. A two-for-one sale? Tickets to the Celtics? Actually, business guru Tom Peters was coming to town and the gray-and-blue-clad businesspeople were snatching the flyers up.

Want to see another example? Head for Appendix B.

Chapter

11

Newsletters

Have your priority list out? If you're just starting a marketing campaign, put this one at the bottom. I'm not suggesting that newsletters aren't valuable. They can help immensely, giving customers useful tips, provocative coupons, and a positive image of you. Even if they don't read every issue, they'll be reminded of you every time it shows up. But your newsletter requires time, focus, skill, and often money—and customers to receive it. Before you invest all these things, make sure your basic market tools are set.

Cost

This depends on the length of your newsletter. The cost of an emailed newsletter is free if you do it yourself, but the time you spend designing it can be expensive. A better idea might be to use an auto-responder service. These guys have HTML design templates ready—all you do is pick the one you want and plug in the essentials: the content, your logo, and photographs, drawings, or other visuals.

If you go hard copy, the bill is similar to what you'd pay for a brochure. According to Chris Pritchard at OfficeMax, the bill will run you about nine cents per side for a black and white 8.5 x 11. Now for the really bad news: a color 8.5 x 11 is eighty-nine cents per side, and significantly more for 11 x 17. As with brochures and flyers, the price per unit goes down the more you buy.

If you purchase articles for your newsletter, they can run you from fifty dollars each to several hundred for a year's worth of copy. Or you can hire a copywriter, usually for $50 an hour.

Use

Newsletters are as versatile as the content that goes in them. Here are a few possibilities:

• **Coupons and special-offer listings.** Remember we talked about exclusivity with your website? Well, exclusivity works wonders here. Your customers sign up to receive your newsletter knowing that they'll receive special offers available to no one else. When your newsletter arrives, they naturally open it to see what special treats are waiting for them.

• **A tips-based newsletter.** Filled with plenty of the tips we discussed in the last chapter, this newsletter offers helpful advice for your customer and is easy to write for you. Scatter in special offers and news about your business and the industry.

• **The internal newsletter.** If you have more than thirty employees, this is a must. Okay, you may be thinking, why market to your employees? They aren't the customers. But as you'll see later in this book, your employees assert your brand and establish your business as the best around. In fact, they are your principle marketing asset! Your internal newsletter helps underscore your brand and keeps them focused on reflecting the business promise.

Yes, you can distribute newsletters far and wide. But beware. If you spend money producing a thousand for a conference, plenty of people will take one, but realistically, how many will read them? Try to narrow your newsletter distribution to those chosen few—which can number hundreds. Online newsletters can be better than hard copy for a few reasons: customers are more likely to read them, since they're sitting at their desks in an area conducive to reading; the expense and waste involved is far less; and they lend themselves to interesting touches such as flash animation and voice.

What to Do

If you're planning to produce your own newsletter, you have to do it right. That means writing polished, albeit short, articles. Here's what you do:

1. Have an interesting and informative opening paragraph. We've discussed this quite a bit. Here are a few more possibilities for your openings:

Facts. Whether numbers, statistics, or percentages, just make sure they're real and supportable. Say you're writing a marketing piece for your recruitment firm. Here's what you might do:

100,000. That's the number of hours the average person devotes to his career in a lifetime. To help you maximize the value of your 100,000 hours, Professional Placements will identify the right positions for you—and help you get them.

Testimonials. Nothing quite beats true-life stories. Keep the rewards clear and, where possible, measurable:

Amazing things can happen in five years. Take Tina Richards. She started her career as an administrative assistant. Today she is manager of Oakdale Associates with eleven employees reporting to her, and she's earning over $100,000 a year. What are the secrets to her career growth? Tina came to Professional Placements, whose targeted advice and extensive network helped her career grow.

Descriptions. Don't think these are reserved for products. They give the customer a mental vision of how your service could help them.

Enter Tina Richards's Oakdale office and you see not only pictures of her two sons or the view overlooking a pond. You see plaques and awards—all new. In just five years, Tina Richards soared from administrative assistant to manager, earning recognition as she went. All this thanks, in part, to Professional Placements.

2. Add more information in two or three short paragraphs.

Limit your paragraphs to five or six lines, using bullets, lists, whatever it takes to give your structure punch. Here are some other possibilities:

Sidebars, call-outs, and pull-quotes. You know sidebars and call-outs. They're those little boxes at the side of your articles, usually shaded or in a different font than the rest of the piece. Well, it's a sound-bite age, and sidebars and call-outs give your articles an edge that will keep the customer engaged in your newsletter. Especially good: old-fashioned tips, reminders, or step-by-steps your customer can cut and use. Remember the mantra: think usability. As for pull-quotes: they're quotes that you "pull" from the main article and place in a box with quotes around them. By repeating the line, you give emphasis to the meaning, and have an interesting sound bite that encourages the customer to pay attention.

Titles and subtitles. You see titles and subtitles a lot in newspapers and magazines—they break up the structure and act as hooks to get your customer to continue reading. Remember to keep them snappy.

3. Close out.

If you think you need a fancy closing, forget it. Your piece should end naturally. If you want to sum up your thoughts, go ahead—but keep it short!

Newsletter Visuals

The success of your newsletter depends on strong visuals. To get ideas, look through magazines. In some ways, they're a grand-scale version of a newsletter. And since they're in the business of making money, they know precisely what style and content their primary customer appreciates. Here are a few more visual pointers:

• Place your pull-quote within the paragraph, not along the margin or below the article. The customer should be clear of its origin. Also, do not put your call-outs or sidebars parallel to the article; always set them off somehow. For ideas, look at just about any magazine at the newsstand—from *Redbook* to *Time*. Publishers do a great job positioning paragraphs so you're tempted to read every one.

• Use a screen box or horizontal lines to set off your pull-quotes, call-outs, and sidebars. When using a sidebar with tips or more general information, include an interesting header of some sort.

• Use a different font or shading to offset call-outs and sidebars for greater variety. With pull-quotes, enlarge the quotation marks as well.

• Remember, size equals importance in your customer's eye. So prioritize: the more important or interesting visuals should be larger than the rest.

• Make the right decision about your email format. Ideally, provide your customers with a choice of formats to ensure they can open the newsletter and get the full benefit of your great design. Granted, this option takes more time. So, if it's not for you, consider HTML. It's spiffy and has the look and feel of a web page, although some customers may not be able to access it. Otherwise, go simple and use plain text.

Feel overwhelmed but don't have the funds to hire a newsletter designer? Plenty of software programs out there will help—all for under $100. Or hire a designer to set up a newsletter template. When you're ready, just plug in the content and go!

QUICK Tip

Need More? Check out www.about.com. They have articles and helpful tips about creating a newsletter and plenty more for your marketing efforts. Have a great idea? Tips that you think will interest the public? Consider about.com as your own marketing forum and submit what you have.

More Strategies

Use voice. How about welcoming the customers to your newsletter when they access it on your website? Or tell the readers about it on your home page and let them know how they can subscribe.

Add flash! As in Flash animation. Flash can be intriguing and exciting, and it keeps up with your customers' expectations for speed and pizzazz.

Stay consistent. Send it regularly: every day, week, month, or even every other month. If you want real recognition, don't send a newsletter twice a year. Your customers will think you just decided to send it for the heck of it and not take it as seriously.

Build it in! If you're emailing your newsletter, build it into the email itself. Start with the first paragraph of each article with a link leading customers to the rest. Put your special offers, upcoming events, or other "ads" for your business in the margins.

QUICK Tip

The Evergreen/Hot News Difference

Evergreens: Information, such as tips, that you can use any time. Write up a few, and cut and paste them if news is short.

Hot news: Announcements, sales, anything that's time-sensitive and that the customer needs to know now. Feature these on page one.

QUICK Tip

Newsletter Extras

• **Internet links.** The new, the unusual, the helpful. Know a company that provides complementary services your customer would like? Does it have a link to your site? Think karma and include its link in your newsletter as a thank-you. Be sure it really will prove helpful to your customer, of course!

• **Book and movie reviews.** Naturally, these pertain to your field and are of prime interest to your customer. You can give a two-paragraph review or just have an "editor's pick" column.

• **Jokes.** Appropriate and professional. As call-outs, hooks, or part of your article.

• **Updates on professional issues.** An advance in the field? New research? Your customer may be well-informed, but too busy to stay up-to-date. So do it for him. Include a link or point him to where he can go for more.

• **Product reviews.** What do you think? What should she think? Include prices and information about where she can go to purchase or learn more.

Want to see some article samples? Go to Appendix B!

Chapter 12

News Releases and Other Forms of Publicity

The value of a news release depends entirely on your message. It must be timely. It must be interesting. And it must *not* be advertising. Let the content dictate where your news releases lie on your priority list.

Cost

The cost is only your time, if you want to go it alone. But remember, big newspapers usually get enough news releases to cover the office walls in a single day, so the competition for their attention is fierce. This means your release must be competitive and highly polished. So consider investing in a professional news release writer who knows the right release format, and may even know an editor or two. The fee ranges, but is around $350 for each release.

Distribution is another matter. You can send the release yourself to target newspapers. In this case, the price is free. If you want to scatter them far and wide, you need a distribution service. Some, such as PR Free (www.PRFree.com), cost you nothing. Others, such as PR Newswire (www.prnewswire.com), charge a membership fee of $125 and hundreds to thousands of dollars depending on how many releases you want to send. More in a minute.

Use

The news release has numerous functions, not solely to get a newspaper to cover your story. You can place it on your website under the Press Room section, if you like, or include it with your marketing materials folder along with your product listing or clips of articles written by or about your company. Then, there's the more obvious benefit of press releases: they get you great free publicity. In the best of all worlds, a reporter will call for an in-depth interview. Or the editor might cut and paste your release directly into the paper and present it as an article.

A word of caution: a single article rarely brings in earth-shattering results. Usually, the result is fifteen minutes of fame—unless you "market your marketing." Once that article hits the newsstands, let everyone know about it. Email it to customers. Put it on your website. If you own a shop or restaurant, clip it and put it in your window. Going to a conference? Blow up the article and turn it into a poster-size sign, clip and photocopy it and add it to your marketing materials, or leave flyer-size pages for customers to take.

QUICK Tip

Keep Your Clips: When you're clipping an article, just cut it out of the paper and glue it onto another piece of paper. Also, cut out the newspaper's name and the publication date, and glue that at the top. If you're putting the clip in a folder—especially if you expect lots of press in the future—laminate the clip or get plastic covers to avoid the wear and tear of fingers flipping through them.

What to Do

Unlike the other copy we've discussed so far, you have less room for creativity when writing news releases. That makes it doubly tough—you're competing with hundreds of similar releases newspapers receive each day, and you can't rely on the power of your brand or originality to make a competitive difference. So you must master the art of writing a news release, making yours that much better and more newsworthy than the rest.

Most important, maintain an interesting angle and use clean, strong writing: something even professional news release writers neglect. Before you start writing, though, ask yourself if you really need the release. The answer is "yes" if all the following criteria apply:

- Is your idea timely—meaning you must get it out now?
- Will it interest the paper's readers?
- Does it contain something new—or even better, something unexpected?
- Does it connect to some event—local, national, seasonal, or otherwise?

Then, answer this question: is your news release a sales pitch? If your answer is "yes," don't send! (By "sales pitch," I don't mean an announcement saying you opened a new office. That's of great interest to the reader, who might need your product or service.)

Next, determine how to give your release that important customer-focus. In this case, your customer is the newspaper's reader and the editor.

Say you're writing a news release about your company's new website. This is a great idea, especially if your site has a utilitarian component such as online shopping, tip sheets, weekly "lessons," or anything your customers can use. Sure, you want to tell the world your site is up, but focus on the many benefits it brings to visitors.

Then, write the six sections of your release:

1. The top

This contains essential information: your letterhead, the date, the contact person's name (although some companies put that at the bottom of the release), the location, the words FOR IMMEDIATE RELEASE, and a header announcing the point of your message. Here's how it looks:

Stanson & Stanson, Financial Advisors

FOR IMMEDIATE RELEASE

Contact Person: Nick Pryer

(301) 555-9876

nick.pryer@s&s.com

New Website Lets Investors Access Information in Record Time

NEW YORK, January 8, 2007

2. The lead

This first paragraph contains the Five W's: the Who, What, When, Where, and Why of your release. Let's get back to that website idea. You may want a traditional opening, where you say:

NEW YORK, January 8, 2007—Today, Stanson & Stanson, Financial Advisors introduced an online tool that lets their clients get in-depth information about all aspects of their investments immediately.

Or to add a little zip, try writing:

NEW YORK, January 8, 2007—Information is power. And now, investors are stronger than ever with Stanson & Stanson, Financial Advisors' online tool that gets them in-depth information in record time.

Both address the:

Who: Stanson & Stanson, Financial Advisors and clients

What: Can access a sophisticated tool

When: Now

Where: On the Web

Why: To gain information faster

3. The quote

This may be the hardest part of your news release to write; even professional writers struggle with it. The reason: most releases contain made-up quotes from CEOs, employees, and others. A PR writer sends them the quote and they sign off on it. So why is this a problem? Because your quote needs to sound credible and natural, as if someone actually said it, and didn't make it up—a hard goal to reach. Look at the difference:

Someone wrote it: The intrinsic value of this website lies in a navigational system that allows appropriate information to reach individual visitors. This facilitates a faster flow of information overall.

Someone said it: With the website, different investors can get different types of information without having to search for it. This often means they can get information two or three times faster.

4. A narrative paragraph with details

Now add the less important but still significant details—maybe compare the site's functionality to others like it or add an interesting but not central feature. For example, you might say something like this:

The website is the first of its kind since it retrieves highly specific information in seconds, a feat rivaled only by major search engines. The information is broader than customers usually find, as well: they can learn about stock histories and changes in the company, and even access key parts of a CEO's most recent speech.

By the way, make sure your narrative focuses on the customer. This holds true even if you're sending a news release or notice about an event your organization is hosting. Notice how this paragraph . . .

Dudley's Buick will be hosting an Auto Safety Day at the Westchester Mall. This event promises to be one-of-a-kind, with interactive web presentations and guest speakers, including Registry of Motor Vehicles Director Todd Hall.

. . . is more customer-focused like this:

Now, Westchester residents can learn information vital to the safety and well-being of their family at Auto Safety Day at the Westchester Mall. Sponsored by Dudley's Buick, this event promises to be one-of-a-kind, with interactive web presentations and guest speakers, including Registry of Motor Vehicles Director Todd Hall.

5. Second quote, usually a testimonial or customer statement

This gives credibility to your claims by letting someone other than you support it. If you have a new business or are announcing a new service, you can't find someone to say how great your business is—they haven't used it yet. But they can comment on your other offerings, or say how much the community or industry needs what you can provide them with. If all else fails, use a narrative with even more detail or, possibly, skip this paragraph altogether. Let's look at that website news release again:

"My employees were part of the group who tested this product initially. We were amazed at how quickly we could find information for our clients. We figured that saved us fifty thousand dollars or more of employee work time each year," said Harold Dickens, CEO of Financial Services, Inc.

6. The closing bio

Remember that one-paragraph bio you drafted of your business earlier? Stick it in here. Make sure you put the information most critical to your brand up front.

QUICK Tip

Hang Out in Press Rooms: Cruise the Web! Many websites have a press room where they stash their press releases over the years. The good news is that lots of them are interesting, exciting, and well worth learning from. The other good news is that even more are terrible, the language so dry you think your eyes might shrivel up reading them. So, why is this good news? Because you have lots of possibilities for sending one infinitely better.

SPREADING THE WORD

So how do you get your news release out? There are two basic ways:

1. Send the releases to a distribution channel. They can send hundreds of releases to specific locations: national, regional, or trade publications. Like everything else in marketing, follow-up is key. Sadly, most of the distribution services provide no follow-up calls whatsoever. Whether the editor likes your release idea, or even sees it, is anyone's guess. If you hire a PR writer, she'll write the release, find the distribution channel, and follow up.

2. Pick and choose core publications you want to attract, and send your news release to them. To ensure your news release gets into print (or picked up, as they say), you need to remember a few facts. First, the closer you get to the editor the better, which means immediately after you send your release, you or someone else must contact the editor or a key reporter to see if he got your release and is interested in covering your story.

Also, like everything else, the newspaper world is based on networks and personal relations. If you make the calls, remember the editor's name. Next time you have a release to send, address it to that person. When you call back, ask for that person. If you hire a PR person, make sure she is already networked in.

Finally, remember reporters have beats and yours might be on one of them. Every time you read the paper, look for articles about your subject matter. Jot down the reporter's name. Then, when you have something that's newsworthy, alert that particular reporter.

Bringing in the Pros: Bang for your buck? Almost free? Not even close. PR firms charge a good deal of money, can't promise you high exposure, and definitely can't promise you any new business at all. Most firms, and even full-time PR agents who go solo, charge a monthly fee of around $5,000— many want a six- or even twelve-month commitment, which certainly won't help your cash flow any. That's different, by the way, from a person who happens to write news releases for around $300 a pop. So, given this, who should use a PR firm? Generally, a large corporation with constant image issues to manage and competitors clamoring for a front-page spot.

Head for Appendix B for another news release example.

Other Publishing Options

Opinion Pieces

These are the best in free marketing—newspapers lend credibility your own material can't and make you an instant expert. Here's what you do: every time you see an issue in the news that directly relates to your area of expertise, write a short essay that comments on it. Be sure to include as many facts and figures as possible and stick to your point. Do not discuss your business or the services you provide unless they directly connect to your point. This is not an opportunity to advertise. It is an opportunity to comment on relevant information. Naturally, keep your writing strong and your voice professional.

Then, send your piece to the opinion editor at the newspaper of your choice. You can find that person's name just by calling, or you can use a distribution service. In the opinion world, the service is free, but they will review your piece for quality and may or may not take it. Knight Ridder/Tribune is good, but so are plenty of others.

Important: Before you send your opinion piece, review samples from your paper so you give them the style and length they want. And make it timely! If you're commenting on something that appeared in the news on Monday, have your piece out by Wednesday at the latest.

Want to see an opinion piece? Go to Appendix B.

Letter to the Editor

They're short, they're sweet, and if they're not, the newspaper will edit them and still run them if the message is strong enough. Letters to the editor don't have the credibility of articles or opinion pieces, but they will get you exposure. And newspapers publish lots of them, so the chances you'll get published are higher than opinion pieces. Check your local paper to learn about the requirements for sending them in.

The Press Kit

I'm going to say something here that might seem a little unlikely, but here goes: don't bother with a press kit. Unless you're planning to launch a career as a celebrity, or your marketing campaign requires that you're positioned as an expert, you don't need one. If you do, you probably should work with a professional to put it together. Here's what you should include:

- One-page bio about you and/or your business
- One page of testimonials from clients and/or experts in your field
- Photo of you, or the business if it's interesting
- A press release or two that address the issues you want the reporter to cover
- Information about your offerings
- Clips of articles you've written and that have been written about you
- A list of questions for the reporter to ask in an interview
- Schedule information about upcoming events, talks, or other matters

Put the kit in a professional-looking folder. Don't try for glitzy or slick, since that can seem pretentious; the sturdy office supply store variety works great.

QUICK Tip

Take the Bull by the Horns: Everything I've told you so far is tried and true. Now, try some things that aren't tried. If you see a story idea waiting to happen, call the editor and suggest it. Or if you have an opinion on a hot topic that relates to your area of expertise, let the editor or reporter know and offer to give an expert's quote. Have a great idea for an article? Try writing it yourself. Follow the leads you have inside your head—they could be your best PR agent.

Determine which newspaper or magazine your customers are most likely to read. Then, every day, carefully read the sections that are best for you— record the reporters' names, too. Eventually, opportunity will spring up, and you'll know just who to contact and the kinds of angles they're after. Before you know it, you'll find yourself in print.

Chapter 13

Advertising: From Newspapers to the Airwaves and TV

Don't make the mistake of other small businesses and rush into advertising first. It ranks lower than most of your other marketing materials, and costs more. But when coupled with other ventures, advertising can work its way up your priority list.

By the way, test several advertising ideas and stay on the low side budget-wise until you're sure something clicks. Also, make sure your timing's right. Are you an expert? Do people recognize your business name? Your logo? Now's the time to invest in an ad. Customers already know you and will be more attentive to your message, whether it's a special offer or a reminder to call you.

Cost

Depends on the size, length of time you advertise, and the venue. A small ad in your local paper can cost you $300 a month while a billboard ad can cost $5,000 or more a month. The cost of producing the ad also varies. Naturally, you can develop it yourself using a software package, clip art, or other tool. Most newspapers are happy to develop ads for you, but be sure you do a quality check before it goes to press. The price is either free or negligible. Hire an ad agency and the price can be thousands of dollars.

Use

Advertising serves some great functions, but if your business is new, don't expect an ad to immediately lure people in. Your customer needs to see your ad again and again for it to make an impression. So don't plan on a one-day advertisement paying off: commit yourself to several months, at least.

Naturally, you'll get the biggest bang for your advertising buck by piggybacking on other efforts. Planning to speak at a conference? Set up a booth at a local event? Or maybe you were interviewed by your local paper? This is the time to launch your advertisement. Of course, if you're having an extraordinary sale, advertisements can alert the public to really great savings. If this sale happens to be on Memorial Day or Labor Day, you'll obviously have tougher competition from other ads, so try for unusual times or unique offers.

QUICK Tip

The Basics: Although ads are probably the most creative marketing tools around, they have less credibility than articles or seminars where you speak out as an expert, or brochures where you provide tips and testimonials that prove your case. Everyone knows that ads are self-serving and they're too short and immediate to prove otherwise. So, you must give them some sort of entertainment value and emotional connection that the customer will notice and remember.

What to Do

Let's start with the seven ad basics.

1. Make sure your ad revolves around one central image or idea. Perhaps you're having a sale. Have lots of items with prices slashed? Focus on the most enticing one for your primary client, and mention the others in a few words, like "Lots More!" If you're a realtor, don't focus on the fact that you exist. Not good enough—lots of realtors exist. What makes you different? Perhaps your tagline can help you there. Or perhaps you specialize in old homes, upscale buildings, or a particular kind of commercial real estate. That's what your primary clients most need to see.

2. Make it fast. Apply the fifty-millisecond concept here and make that instant impression strong. Have a strong image. Make it funny, beautiful, ironic, or luscious—whatever your brand allows. And keep those words sharp and those sentences short.

3. Make it snappy. Snappy images, quick jokes, catchy photos. Humor, by the way, works wonders (as you probably know from the advertisements you love most). Or, be daring. Try for something that goes against the grain. You can do this tastefully, too. Just think about the recent spate of GEICO ads—as humorous as they were surprising. Or Dove soap, who startled the world by claiming their soap was for real women: round-bellied and somewhat overweight, as we saw.

4. Make it timely. Unless your ad is on a billboard, where a lease can run six months or a year, make your ad timely. If you're touting a sale, make sure you limit it to a specific time frame. If you have a restaurant or other retail outlet but are not having a sale, then connect your ad to something seasonal. Summer reading? Special New Year's dinners? All of these work.

5. Think people. Think action. Yes, put people in your ads—they attract more attention than ads that don't. And yes, include your product. That's a given. But you'll really maximize your ad by showing people using your product or service. But think action. People standing around will make your customer walk away.

6. Keep it narrow. Advertise in those places where your primary customer will see it. Even if you're advertising in the local newspaper, pick your section, and the day when you advertise, carefully. If you're going to advertise on radio, pick a prime time when your customer will hear you. Of course, the commuter hours are more expensive than, say, the wee hours of morning, so you need to factor that in, too. Regardless, the salespeople can surely help you.

7. Cut deals. Salespeople at radio stations, newspapers, and ad agencies are like salespeople everywhere—they'll negotiate. See what sorts of deals are available for you. If you're willing to make a six-month commitment—and you know the advertising will work—they'll probably slash prices dramatically. Either way, it can't hurt to ask.

Now, let's take a look at some of the specific types of ads and what you most need to know about them.

Print Ads

You have lots of options here. Your first step is to search. Naturally, you want to determine which publication is best for your ad and your budget. The *Wall Street Journal* might be ideal, but unless you have mega-capital for marketing, one small ad might eat up your reserve. And remember, one ad one time probably won't help.

Once you select the publication, walk through it and look at the kind of ads that are available. Then, sit down with the sales representative and discuss your options. Look at the ads they put together for other companies. Consider the expense and wisdom of making your own ad and sending it to the publisher. And remember, ask about these possibilities:

- Special editions, focusing on your industry
- Inserts that will highlight your business
- Classified ads
- Dates of special events where the publisher might have a booth and give away a higher than usual volume of newspapers

Shop Around: To check the wisdom of placing your ad in a particular newspaper, do this: look for ads from companies that are similar to yours but aren't competitors. Then call or drop by the establishment and ask the owners about their ad experience. How long before the ad started bringing in business? What size ad worked best? And did they cut any deals with the editor for costs? Then make your decision.

QUICK Tip

By the Numbers: Supposedly you'll reach 25 percent more readers with a two-page ad than a one-page ad, and around one-third more readers with a full-page ad than a half page.

Radio Ads

Radio ads have a certain appeal. They can give business owners their fifteen minutes of fame and give their business a certain amount of credibility that's built into the airwaves. Airtime costs vary depending on the time of day—certain times are more expensive than others. Go for a local station at off-hours, and the cost is reasonable. Go with a big affiliate like CBS at prime time or "drive time," and the cost will be dizzyingly steep.

Here are some decisions you'll need to make:

• **The station's listener.** You might love jazz, but your customer may be firmly into rock and roll. So you need to consider their tastes when selecting a venue. Here are some of the options:

> **Top 40:** This is younger, very bubblegum. You need an energetic ad.

> **All talk:** These are usually politically charged and hot to handle.

Progressive rock: Don't rule out the college crowd and small nonprofits. They accept sponsors, if not ads.

All news: Listen closely before you advertise, and make sure your message won't fade in the din.

Classical: Remember both the commercial and public radio versions.

• **The hours that they listen**. If you're targeting working professionals, 7 p.m. to 10 p.m. may be best. But college students are known to listen into the wee hours of dawn. Anyway, radio stations set their clock to time slots, not individual hours. Here's what they are:

6 a.m. to 10 a.m. Known as "a.m. drive time," this coveted slot has the most listeners. They're receptive—usually because they're sitting in their cars driving to work with nothing else to do.

10 a.m. to 3 p.m. The listeners drop off in the midday slot. The ones that stay tuned are often listening while they work. They're loyal, though, and so are their coworkers who might be listening too.

3 p.m. to 7 p.m. The "p.m. drive time" hours have almost as large an audience as the morning hours and listeners stay tuned for the same reason.

7 p.m. to 6 a.m. During these hours, your customer may be busy with other things, among them watching TV and sleeping. But if your customer is a shift worker at a factory or hospital, this could be prime time for you and significantly cheaper than the other slots.

• **Love at fifth sight considerations**. In radio terms, that's frequency. And the big question: How often each day should your customer hear your message over weeks or months? Stations measure frequency by the week, so you need to think in clusters of time. Another consideration: How long do you want your ad to be? A fifteen-, thirty-, or sixty-second segment? Regardless, for your ad to have any effect at all, you need to air it over and over.

• **Music or background sounds**. You may want classical music or bird calls, a comic sound like a dog barking, or the sounds of someone strangely out of breath. The sound should match your brand and help support the mood of your message. No birds chirping or soft classical if you're trying to drum up excitement about your new offering.

• **Voice**. If you want to be the voice for your own message, just make sure you can pull it off. Most people's voices fall flat or they sound like they're reading a script—not exactly compelling. Since you're not going live, you can try and try again in the station studio. But remember two things: you must get that same instant emotional response from the customer as you do in print, and voice modulation is key.

QUICK Tip

More Ways to Hit the Radiowaves: The power of remote! Having a grand opening or sponsoring an event? The station will send an announcer to give periodic broadcasts from your location. Some stations even send a disc jockey to do the show live.

You can always act as a sponsor, too. Why not consider NPR, if you have professional customers? You'll be doing a public service and your listener will equate you with a station that is reliable and intelligent. Or sponsor a news, weather, sports, or traffic report on a Top 40 or Golden Oldies station.

Your customer will hear your business' name before and after the report, as in: "This weather report is being brought to you by Carlson's Clothes," with a quick tagline or description of what you do, as in: "makers of quality clothing for big and tall men." Most stations sweeten the deal with a ten- or fifteen-second commercial adjacent to the report and a thirty- or sixty-second commercial during the day.

Remember: Planning to air a radio ad? See how your other campaigns will support it.

Billboards

Really great billboards attract really great attention. But whether or not you're a candidate for a billboard depends on numerous factors. Here are a few. If you answer yes to all these questions, go ahead.

• **Can you afford it?** The price of a billboard can range from around $600 to $5,000 or more a month, which is more than almost any other marketing endeavor except radio or TV. Can your advertising budget withstand this expense?

• **How broad is your customer base?** If you own a restaurant, it's pretty broad; after all, people have to eat, and a billboard may bring hungry travelers in. If you own a boutique, a specialty shop, or almost any kind of consulting firm that targets distinct professions, better spend your money in other ways.

• **Do you have the right location, location, location?** If your business is in close proximity to the sign, or is easy to find, indicate on the billboard where drivers should go. If the trip requires lots of turns and is twenty miles down the pike, don't bother.

• **Do you have "billboard-ability"?** Does your offering lend itself to a snappy, eye-catching design? Remember, your customer is speeding past, giving your sign a millisecond or so of attention. The image must be sharp and memorable, providing them with an instant reason to come in.

• **Is your cash flow good?** Normally you have to reserve a billboard months or more in advance, with a commitment that's stronger than marriage. So think cash flow. Will you have the money on hand to pay for the billboard a year or so from now?

If you answered "yes" to all these questions, hop in your car and drive to the spot where you'd like your billboard to be. Then, look at the bottom of the billboard that's currently there for the name of the outdoor advertising company and give them a call. That specific billboard may not be available, but they can give you a map of others in your area.

In terms of the actual design, the billboard company or a designer (probably at a lower price) can create one for you. Be sure to show them your materials so they can get a real sense of your brand. And beware—these guys are in the design business, so be sure to find someone who's familiar with yours.

Television

Thanks to the wonders of television, you can reach your target group when they're feeling relaxed and willing to hear your message. For most small businesses, television is well beyond the reach of their budget. The average price is high, peaking at the Super Bowl's $1 million for a spot. Unless, of course, you opt for cable. The prices can be affordable, sometimes in the hundreds for one minute of airtime, and the production costs of making the ad can be as low as $6,000. By the way, don't worry about numbers of viewers: with television, you're better off reaching fewer customers more often than reaching everyone in the nation at once. Call your local cable company to find out about their audiences.

Other considerations: Does your offering lend itself to the television venue? And is this particular station the best place to reach your primary customer? Even more important, do you want to be associated with the station? If you have a highbrow company and advertise on a lowbrow cable station, the answer is no. And, as with billboards, you have to determine if your customer base is broad enough to merit the effort.

If so, what kind of music and image do you want? You need a great spokesperson for your business. Should that person be you? Like all advertising, you need to advertise again and again. Do you want to make that commitment?

If television seems like the right choice for you, here are a few more tips:

• More often is better than more people. I said this already, but it's worth a second look. Otherwise, you're throwing your marketing cash straight into the airwaves.

• Most television spots are thirty seconds. These generate leads but don't sell products. For that, a sixty-second spot is significantly better.

• Flash or otherwise state your 800 number on the screen at least three times. Don't have an 800 number? Get one that's easy to remember and closely tied to your offering and your brand.

• Give them something *specific* to respond to: a special sale; a unique event; a new but limited product.

• Shop around for the best production company. Review their other ads. Call their customers and ask if they were easy to work with, customer-oriented, and creative.

Alert!

Don't Go It Alone: The Television Bureau of Advertising (www.TVB.org) has everything you need to know about demographics, pricing, and the newest in television advertising.

QUICK Tip

Easy Research: Now's the time to make the most of lying on the couch! Watch the station that best suits your budget and demographic requirements. Don't bother with the shows—watch the ads. Find some you like? Call the company and see if they'll reveal the secrets, from their scriptwriter to their production company. They might even divulge ways you can get the right price.

QUICK Tip

Other Visual Venues: As always, think outside the box—the television box. With so many specialty stations around, you're sure to find one that matches your product. Sell specialty garden supplies? Try the Home and Garden network. If sports are your thing, so is ESPN. Doubtless, your community has a station announcing school closings, football game times and locations, and other local events. If you own a local business, your customer is waiting.

Then there's the Check-out Channel and the Airport Channel: all part of the growing "place-based" marketing. You see them flashing in every airport waiting area, travelers watching, transfixed.

Chapter 14

Giveaways

Unlike other marketing materials, like business cards or a website, whether you invest in giveaways depends entirely on your marketing strategy. If you have a retail business, then the success of your grand opening can depend on giveaways. In other cases, they can be extra or unnecessary. Your best bet: read the following chapter that explores when you might use your giveaways, and what those items might be, and then decide.

Cost

The price depends on the item. With computer programs, you can actually design your own calendars, assemble your own handbooks, and develop your own posters. But beware: a cheap-looking or broken product reflects badly on your business. And think bulk; as always, the more you buy, the more the cost diminishes.

Then, think design. According to Craig Davidiuk of Ultimate Promotions, the price depends on many variables. A mug, for example, can start at a dollar and go to six dollars. Pens can cost two dollars apiece. But as Davidiuk says, "If you want to buy a cheap pen, go to Wal-Mart, buy as many as you need, and put your name on the envelope." If you want a pen that's quality and plays up your brand, go for the best.

Use

Giveaways can either really boost your marketing endeavor or be a complete waste of money, depending on what you give away—and how you market it. Here are some ideas:

• **Enticements.** If you're in retail, giveaways can act as a surefire enticement, getting customers to enter your shop. And they're a definite at any grand opening. Just be sure you publicize what you're giving away so customers are sure to come in.

• **Face-to-face interactions.** Remember, people buy from people. That's your marketing mantra. Every gift you give the customer buys face time with you. Your impulse might be to tout your product, and that's fine. But use your face time to talk about the customer, too. Where does he live? How many kids does he have? Whatever is appropriate. This will seal your relationship with him and up the likelihood that he'll return when he needs your product or service. Having a booth at a conference? The same holds true.

• **Reciprocity builders.** Reciprocity, or the concept of "You scratch my back, I'll scratch yours," is a major force in human interaction. You engage in it all the time, although you may not be aware. A colleague takes you out for lunch one week, so you take him out the next. Your friend invites you to a party in the spring; you invite her in the fall. With your business, reciprocity is no mere sales gimmick: it's a way for you to create a natural relationship. You give the customer something, and he gives you loyalty back.

- **On-the-chest advertising**. A Frisbee is great. So is a pen. But Frisbees often get tossed in a closet, never to be seen again. And the pen? The print is so small, even the person using it can't see it. But a T-shirt? A baseball cap? These get maximum exposure in all the right places. Sure, they remind the customer that you're out there in the world, but they also alert everyone else that you're out there, too. And remember the love at fifth sight idea? These could be the one-two-three of advertising your brand.

What to Do

There are countless ways to approach giveaways. We'll look at a few of them. But before we do, a few reminders. First, remember the usability factor. Make sure your giveaway serves a central purpose. Take calendars. Sure, everyone needs a calendar. And plenty of businesses give them away once December begins. And, yes, your customers will glance at them all year round, especially if the image is good. But will they regularly use them? And think of you appreciatively when they do?

The answer is yes if you include reminders on key days of the month so the customer comes to rely on the calendar, not simply view it. For example, at the beginning of the book, I mentioned my calendar from the West Virginia Extension Service. It indicates days of the month I need to feed my house plants, order seeds, plant seeds indoors—I look at the calendar constantly. By the way, it doesn't contain any ads or reminders of how helpful the service is. It doesn't have to—the calendar does the job.

Second, make sure your giveaway suits your business purpose. A sports supply store that gives away teddy bears with little baseball hats may be an adorable concept, but will it sell cleats and bats? Third, put your logo, business name, and web address in a (tastefully) visible place. You can use that space, by the way, to advertise other giveaways. If you operate a movie theater, you may want to sell booklets of coupons. That may be just the place to announce other giveaways, like a free soda with every order of a large popcorn and box of candy.

So, here are a few places where giveaways can prove a great advantage:

Grand openings. Publicize your giveaways—door prizes, raffle rewards, or free services—in your advertisements, in your window display, and just about everywhere else. If you have an office with lots of pedestrian traffic, sweeten the deal by displaying one of the products they could win.

Daily customers. Have a sign by your guestbook: "Want to be on our mailing list for special offers? Free gifts? Sign up here!" Have room for their email address, which you'll use later when you publicize that first sale, upcoming event, or free gift.

Lotteries. This is where customers put their name on a ticket and you spin, spin, spin. A few caveats: Show them the prizes, so the reward becomes more enticing. And don't offer just one. Three is the usual number, but go for even more. A happy winner will be a certain customer. And get his email address and add it to your mailing list. If he doesn't supply this information, and you pull his ticket, he must be the winner anyway.

Contests. You know the routine. Jellybeans in a jar. Pennies in a container. These work well, as customers really need to think. But be inventive. If you happen to be a landscaper, how about using pea pebbles? If you operate a day care center, try children's buttons. You can also hold contests where customers suggest names for your new product or taglines for a campaign. Post the winners and their pictures on your website and store wall, and announce them in an ad or a press release in your local paper. You'll have a great name for your product and the winners (and their friends) will join your other customers to purchase it!

Bits and Pieces

Not sure about what to give away? Before we close this section, let's take a look at some possibilities.

Pens and Pencils

These are the most common because they're relatively inexpensive: as low as a dollar each. They're easy to lug into conferences and offer in a fishbowl or other container to clients entering your office. But as I've mentioned, they're easy to lose and tend to be of questionable quality.

Bumper Stickers

This is not the time to be modest. Your name and logo should travel through the nation—or the world. Politicians have them, and who are they? Trust me, you offer a much better deal. If you can, find something humorous or catchy. To this day, I remember one bumper sticker I saw years back in New England for a seafood restaurant called Bertha's. It read: "Eat Bertha's Mussels." Attention-getting, isn't it?

Clothing

Obviously, we're not talking cardigan sweaters here. But you can give caps, T-shirts, and other garments away to your favorite customers at grand openings or other events. Naturally, you want your logo, company name, phone number, and/or web address on the shirt—tastefully done, of course. No one wants to be a walking billboard, but with the right positioning, your logo can be cool, upscale, hip, smart—whatever you're aiming for. Think Hard Rock Café.

T-shirts will run you about ten dollars apiece, although that depends on the quantity, color, and other factors. Another idea: use your T-shirt as an incentive to anyone purchasing over a certain amount, or give T-shirts as prizes at your grand opening. Also consider marketing from within: give your employees T-shirts as Christmas gifts (hopefully along with a bonus!).

Calendars

We've talked about these already. They're great because the customer has a good reason to keep them. We mentioned indicating dates when your customer should take a specific action. Also, consider adding a tip, or several tips, of the month. If your brand allows it, try humor, too. A joke of the month? A pun every third or fourth day? These work wonders.

Videos

The video, of course, can be of you or some other representative of your business who can strike a really great pose. These can work wonders if you provide information invaluable to the customer. Own a health club? How about a video that complements your fitness program, like how to prepare healthy and nutritious food? Are you an attorney? How about walking new business owners through the forms they need to complete to get started?

If you want to share the production costs, find a partner to join you. She'll also share the spotlight, but no matter. Both of you will be distributing the video, which will give you twice the distribution bang for the buck. For example, that health club could partner with a medical clinic and provide advice on everything from posture to eating the right foods to ward off cancer.

Free Samples

If you own any kind of food or beverage establishment, definitely hand out samples. You have the chance to chat and bond with customers as they stand around and eat. Plus, they'll sign your guestbook and get on your mailing list. They are eating your food, after all. And hopefully they'll like what they taste and want to buy some of it. If not, reciprocity will kick in and they'll buy something else. Remember, think outside of the box. Own a gourmet food store? How about an olive oil tasting? A pizzeria? How about samples of new and inviting pizza combinations?

Posters

Here's what you do. Find a really great piece of artwork: a photo, a drawing (without copyright restrictions), or even your logo, if it's really good. Blow it up to a poster size, with your business name and possibly the city where you're based at the bottom. Tuck your web address and phone number in a corner; don't let it distract from the image. People will take them home, put them up, even frame them. Tourists will love them as souvenirs, and return to your place later or order from you online because you're fresh in their memory. Why not get one framed and offer it to a contest or raffle winner?

Selling plus

In the back of your mind, think sales. Yes, you can sell those posters. And T-shirts. And lots of your giveaways, provided they're good enough. This will enhance their value when you offer them as prizes later, too.

QUICK Tip

Getting Services Noticed: If you provide a service, the task of maximizing your giveaway power is harder since your customer probably doesn't enter your establishment very often, if at all. So, you need to reserve your giveaways for holidays (although many organizations no longer accept gifts) or conferences and other events. If this is the case, up the usability factor by a thousand. You'll be competing with hundreds of other vendors with countless other giveaways, and you don't want yours sinking to the bottom of someone's brown paper bag, lost among the many.

Alert!

Know the Law: If you're planning to have a contest, special offer, or event, make sure you're doing it legally. For example, the practice of selling lottery tickets or other games based on luck is illegal. So is refusing to provide a sale item once the sale ends if you didn't identify the closing date in writing. For more, consult the Direct Marketing Association (www.the-dma.org) and have a lawyer review anything you put in writing.

CASE STUDY: AND THE GIVEAWAY AWARD GOES TO . . .

Harry Rauner, president of Virginia-based Business Bank, has an imaginative and enticing take on the giveaway. His bank hosts weekly "brunch-lunches" for guests from nearby businesses and special "Lunch with Harry" affairs for valued customers. The menu starts with sausage, eggs, and pancakes, and gravitates to sandwiches, sodas, and chips as the day, and guests, move on. In the summer, the bank even hosts ice cream socials.

But the impressive angle is not the food (although it does attract up to 175 employees and their bosses) but the giveaways. Granted, some aren't exactly "free" in the classic sense, but they'll have greater value than a baseball cap and won't get lost in the seat cushions like a pen. Here's a short list:

- Special deals on safe deposit boxes

- Free orders of checks

- CDs at special rates

In case you're concerned those checks will wilt in the rain, not to worry. Business Bank also gives away free umbrellas, and not the cheap fold-up kind destined to break.

QUICK Tip

Check This Out: Get online and mosey on over to the Advertising Specialties Institute at www.ASIcentral.com. This site is designed for suppliers as well as customers, and it offers as much information about what to give—and who to give it to—as you'll ever need.

Section IV

People, Places, and Things: The Ultimate Marketing

Chapter 15

Telephone Marketing

Everyone hates getting a sales call during dinner. Actually, everyone hates getting a sales call anytime, especially when the voice on the other end is clearly reading a script and seems indifferent to what it's selling. That may make you dismiss telephone marketing from your to-do list. But wait! Telephone sales can be a major boon to your customer base if you do it right, and the cost is just your or an employee's time.

Make it tempting

If you offer people something they don't want, they may consider you a nuisance. But if you call offering something they do want, or even better, something they need, then you're doing them a favor.

So, how do you make the best of the telephone? Here are the ten key steps. When you're done, go to Appendix A, Worksheet 5, Telephone Sales (page 233), and fill in the blanks. Then you should be ready to pick up the phone.

1. Determine Why You're Calling

The reason *why* you're calling should be your primary focus, at first, for any of these reasons:

Selling Something, Right Then, Right There

If this is the primary why behind your call, make sure that telephone marketing is the right way to go. Depending on your product or service, you may want to invest your time and money in other possibilities: events, sales, and good old advertising among them. But yes, you can sell over the phone. No question. Just make sure your item is really hot, as in it's new, few others are touting it, and people will instantly understand and appreciate it. Beware of anything that requires a visual, such as a house, parcel of land, or terrific office space, unless name recognition explains it all.

Also, beware of anything too abstract: five hours of consulting on financial management or investment opportunities requires a certain amount of trust and a greater return on investment than you can articulate on the phone. And speaking of returns on investments, don't expect the customer to purchase anything with a high price tag. That usually requires numerous phone calls, meetings, more meetings, and other efforts. Finally, make sure the customer can pay for it immediately, by credit card, right there on the phone.

Getting People to Show Up at an Event

In many cases, this marketing call can be the most welcome of all. Most events offer more and take less: a grand opening, for example, overflows with giveaways, food, beverages, even bands, and the price (nothing) is right.

If you're offering a seminar or training session with a price tag, you can still promise a great time within a specific time frame. No six-month commitment here: just a one- or two-day session with all the perks. The only hitch: try to get some sort of commitment. Well-meaning people say "yes," but let it fade into "no" later.

Arranging an Appointment

This is another great reason to call. No heavy pressure. No big commitments. You just want to come and meet with a company representative, a department head, or the Big Boss. The appointment strategy works particularly well if you offer a service. If they'll grant you thirty minutes, they're instantly prescreened (they wouldn't waste their time if they had no interest) and the face-to-face time could seal the deal.

If you're making an appointment at someone's home, you can always use the vacuum cleaner sales strategy: offer her something if she meets with you, regardless of whether she buys your product. With the vacuum cleaner, her favorite rug is cleaner, even if she doesn't make the purchase. This is a win-win deal for all: you get the opportunity to display your goods and the prospective customer gets something she wants for her time.

Getting Leads

The immediate purpose of your call is not to get leads—it's to get customers. But the road to marketing can be a long, windy one with plenty of bridges to cross. And those bridges usually take the form of phone calls and more phone calls. This is a good thing. It leads you to more potential customers and more potential leads. And don't forget: if you do it right, a "no" today could easily become a big "yes" tomorrow. So, put "leads" on your list of responses, even if it's not the overwhelming "yes" you want.

2. Determine Who You're Calling—Be Realistic

Who is your audience for the call? The ultimate is someone whose number you got personally, whether through your website, your guestbook, or a referral. If you don't have these, you need to narrow down your target group to those who will love and need you the most. If you're single, you wouldn't go to a club for the happily married. When making calls, don't waste your time on bad choices or uncertainties.

If you're cold-calling business-to-business, you probably want a VP, CEO, or other decision-maker. This is great, but there's one glitch. They're usually protected by gatekeepers: those secretaries, employees, and caller IDs who block the way. So be realistic. Determine who those other people might be, and build a contingency plan into the picture. If it's an administrative assistant, for example, you may want to speak to her frankly. Ask if she thinks her employer is interested in your offering; if not, you certainly won't waste her time. If the gatekeeper is electronic, think about the message you want to leave on the phone. Were you referred by someone? Did they sign up to be on your call list or otherwise present themselves to you? That will be in your plan.

3. Determine Who Is Calling for You

You need to consider who makes these calls and the many pros and cons to each. Take a look:

You

Pros: You know your offering better than anyone. You can answer any question; you can probably *anticipate* any question. And the price—your time—is right. Besides, if you make five or ten calls a day, you don't even have to cut into your energy budget too deeply.

Cons: If you're like most people, you probably hate making marketing calls. It's exhausting, even embarrassing, and the countless no's may seem like personal rejections. And do you really have time for even five or ten calls a day? How much wiser to spend those brief folds in your schedule doing something else.

An Employee

Pros: The employee can devote chunks of his time to making these calls, keeping careful records, and planning a strategy. The employee doesn't have to be dedicated to this activity, either: you can build the calls into his schedule. The upside is the employee gets some variety in his day, plus a bonus and added perk each time a call brings in a deal. If you hire a dedicated caller, you need to decide whether to pay a flat fee, a commission, or both. Your major consideration should be the amount of the sale and the closing time. Contracts can close in a day, weeks, months, or even years.

Cons: The employee doesn't know your business as well as you do. He calls, and he's doing fine in the first few lines, then BAM!—the questions start. Your employee starts to falter. Another problem: the employee may not have the zeal or the vision for follow-up, and, if you have a long closing time, you need that consistency to close the deal.

Call Services

Pros: You and your employees don't have to do it, and can focus on other, more technical matters, like providing the service or making that product you're selling.

Con: Yikes. This can be where the trouble begins. People who know nothing about your offering. People paid to call, call, call, but not to answer questions, strike deals, or think. Besides, they have no relationship with the person. And referrals? None of those, either. Worse, many of them make it far too obvious that they're reading a script.

4. Write Your Script

Scripts are funny things. Yes, you need them. But not in the way a Shakespearean actor needs them. Scripts should guide your phone call and provide cues, but the real thing should come from the interaction between you (or whoever is calling) and the person on the other end of the line. So, when drafting a script you can either write out the whole thing or simply draw up some cues. Either way, be sure that you reflect your brand and focus on that one, compelling offer.

Here's what you must include:

Opening Line

This is the hook we discussed with marketing materials. But because the discussion is live, you have more wiggle room playing off of your customers' responses. Ideally, your opening line will directly connect you to the person on the other end. Note the word directly. If you have a referral, state that first: "Marc Stone suggested that I call." If you're not sure the person will know exactly who Marc Stone is, you can tell them: "Marc Stone of Commerce International suggested that I call."

By the way, this rule applies to just about any referral. For example, say the person from your last call had no interest in your offer. Naturally, you'll ask her if she knows anyone who does. Because you're so friendly and professional, she doesn't want to leave you hanging (literally), so she gives you the name of one or two people in her organization or industry. Then, when you call the referral, let him know who sent you. At the very least, he'll hear you out.

If you got his name from your guestbook or a lottery ticket at your business, then mention that. Try saying: "Hi, this is Sonya from the

Alaska Club. You gave us your number at our open house last month." Or: "You entered our lottery and checked the box that said we can call you, so here we are." In calls of this sort, levity always helps.

But let's say you don't have a referral, and got his name off a list or out of a community or business-to-business phone book. Before you start with a standard "Have I got a deal for you" opening, think about any connection you could make. For example, say your business was recently in your local paper or, even better, a national trade publication, newspaper, or magazine. Try saying: "Yes, I'm calling from the Alaska Club. You probably read about us in *Travel* magazine."

He may not have read *Travel* magazine. But that's not the point. Just mentioning *Travel* magazine immediately gives your business credibility. You may also say: "You may have heard about us from Garett Winderhiem. He writes that column for *Travel* magazine." If an employee is calling on your behalf, try this: "You probably heard of Sonya. Sure, she was in *Travel* magazine last month."

If all else fails, try saying something about yourself. Like: "I'm calling from the Alaska Club. We're the preeminent hiking and tour company for greater Alaska." If he's interested, he'll say something—"uh-huh," "oh," or "cool"—and you can continue. If he's not interested, trust me, you'll know.

Immediate Offer

Your next line should offer him something. Whatever you do, skip the canned stuff. If you've ever gotten a cold call at home, you know exactly what I mean. That's where the caller says, "Is Mr. Stone home, please?" You say, "Yes," and she immediately tries to establish a relationship by becoming chatty, usually saying something like: "How are you today, Mr. Stone?" Naturally, she's reading from a script and you know she doesn't mean it. Besides, who has time to chat with a nameless stranger these days, especially when you'd rather be doing just about anything else?

Instead, make your pitch. Let him know about whatever offer is out there right away. So, you might say, "We're hosting three special tours of Alaska for AARP members at a substantial discount and we thought you might be interested." Or, prequalify him, but make it real: "Are you a member of AARP by any chance?" That's where he says, "Why, yes." And you say, "Great! Well, we're having a package deal for AARP members to take one of our Alaska tours."

By the way, when possible, use the name of another organization to add credibility to your offer. AARP is great—they have more lobbying power than the oil industry, and more members than many small nations. But get their approval first!

Engage Them

Here's where you provide more detail about the excruciatingly wonderful adventure, product, or service that awaits the person at the other end. It's here that you must digress from your script since how you interact with the recipient means everything. Suppose he returns with your dream line: "Oh yes, I've always wanted to go to Alaska! How much is that deal?" Then show how great that deal really is.

More likely, though, you'll get the "Hmm . . . Alaska?" kind of statement. Or possibly some surprisingly innocent comment like "How does the tour get through all that ice?" or "Do they have sunlight in Alaska?" No matter. This is where you talk up the outstanding beauty of Alaska, the marvelous food, and the outdoorsy (but altogether comfortable) hotels where your lucky recipient will stay.

If he says something like, "I hate to travel," or "Alaska? Never liked the place," don't push him. But ask if he knows another AARP member who may be interested.

Seal the Deal

This is where you present your proposition, like: "If you're interested, we can FedEx you a package and you'll get it first thing tomorrow." Or:

"Well, if you like, we can sign you up today for our Alaska Club. There's no commitment involved, but you will get our newsletter, special offers, even a poster of the Alaskan wilderness you'll absolutely love." Whatever you do, make sure your closing has these qualities to sustain your customer's interest after you hang up:

• **Time frame.** Customers are much more inclined to purchase when you have a deadline attached. It creates a sense of urgency that makes them more willing to speed ahead and raises their perception of the value of your offering. Make sure your deadline is authentic: once it ends, it ends.

• **Follow up.** If they want to think about your offer, fine. But make a follow-up plan, like sending them one of your giveaways, getting them on your newsletter list, or telling them about special deals, tips, or other points of interest on your website. If you happen to be discussing something of mutual interest, perhaps send a copy of an article or tell them about a website that addresses the subject.

• **Commitment.** If you can, get a commitment. The ideal is money down, or even better, a full payment. Barring that, try to get an appointment at your customer's office, an agreement that he'll show up for your event (let him know you registered him), or a future time when he'll be happy to talk with you.

• **Suggestion.** If possible, get your customer to suggest next steps. This gives him ownership of the future, and lets you say: "As you suggested, I'm . . ." You can come out and ask him, "What would you like me to do next?" or "Is there anything else you want me to do?" You can build these options into your script, but they'll vary with each phone call.

Closing

Your closing is a chance to repeat your commitment and clarify your next steps. Try to end on a high note. If the answer is a definite "no"— no problem. Ask if he knows anyone else who would appreciate your offer, and hang up.

Don't Waste Time: Please, please, whatever you do, don't spit out an 800 number where people can call you if they have any questions, especially if they're not interested. It doesn't do any good. Besides, what are the odds they're standing around with a pad of paper and pencil in hand, waiting to record your number? This only annoys people.

5. Practice the Script

Yes, you do need to practice. Even more important, so do your employees. Which means even if you don't want to conduct phone calls yourself, you need to spend a day or two making test calls to determine the recurring responses, objections, and questions you might get. Then, have your employees read the script aloud with you playing the role of customer.

Later, you might be tempted to sit in the room as your employee calls, or even tape the interaction. Don't be afraid of a pending lawsuit for eavesdropping—this is perfectly legal as long as the customer knows the conversation is being recorded. The only problem with these scenarios is that your employee might be too self-conscious to let loose and do a good job. In that case, let your employee know that from time to time you'll be listening in. He won't know when, so he'll be relaxed as he calls, you get to check and offer up any suggestions, and all will be well.

6. Call at the Right Time and the Right Place

To maximize the power of your marketing calls, determine the best time to call your customer. (In the office, supposedly first thing in the morning when everyone's perky and bright, and last thing in the day when they're relieved to be going home, are best.) As for the days, rumor has it Tuesday, Wednesday, and Thursday are prime, but never Friday. Who wants to do business on Friday?

More important, apply logic. Some customers may be sitting at their desks at early as 6 a.m. Who calls a business at 6 a.m.? If someone picks up the phone, chances are higher that you'll get the decision-maker— she hasn't started her busy day yet. Other places, especially retail, are open seven days a week, and Monday is usually slowest. Good time to call, don't you think? Given the number of voice mails you'll end up getting, you should easily make twenty or so calls in an hour, maybe more. Consider that when you draft your to-call list.

7. Create a Calling Log

This is critical. Write down the date, time, and person you called, and keep track of the best time to reach him. If you're calling one department and a person there sends you to another, record that. You'll need that person's name for the opening line when you call with the referral. And should you close the deal, you should call or email the person who referred you and say thanks.

Obviously, you'll write down their comments and recommendations for follow-up. But don't forget to add the contents of your conversation. Say the client mentioned he has season tickets to the Red Sox game. You may want to shoot off an email to see if he witnessed a really great game. If the client spends December in Mexico, you can email her a humorous note when you're trapped in a blizzard.

So, make sure your log has these categories:
• Person's name, title, and department
• Time and date you called
• Response in terms of interest
• Elements of your conversation
• Follow-up
• Items you emailed or mailed

8. Practice the Savvy Art of Follow-Up

We talked about follow-up already, but let's dwell for a minute longer. Remember, follow-up is everything, and "no" doesn't always mean "no." Say a customer is interested in your service, gets information, accepts your follow-up calls, and then says "no." Consider that "no" a "maybe," and follow up. Not every week, but consistently. The follow-up can be a quick email, a link to a topic that might interest her, or an invitation. If you have cool giveaways, perhaps send one along. Only because it makes sense to do so, by the way—not as a bribe.

9. Give Them Instant Accessibility Strategies

Make sure that you are accessible. Find an 800 or 888 number that is easy to remember or reflects your brand, as in 1-800-555-TUNE, if you happen to sell CDs. Your website should be obvious by the name of your business—stay as close to the real thing as possible. Is your product available at stores in their community? Will you be attending a conference or other event? Let them know about it during the call and in your follow-up material afterwards.

10. Look into Other Telephone Marketing Possibilities

We talked about 800 numbers a little, but a few more words. Since you have but a nanosecond to reach your customer, make sure your 800 number has punch, and make sure you spell your name correctly or the customer won't remember it. 800 numbers are great for advertisements, too. They're easy for the customer to remember and a painless way for your customer to reach a live person instantly.

And speaking of live people, consider having an old-fashioned call service pick up the phone on weekends or other times. They can let the caller know when you'll return, prioritize the call, find you if necessary, and take messages. Or you can call a service bureau. This is especially useful if you're selling products through TV or radio advertising. These guys will arrange to send the order or just alert you that the order's in.

QUICK Tip

The Three R's of Telephone Marketing

Real: Let the conversation flow naturally; don't force anything.

Right: Don't lie. Ever, ever, ever. Don't even spin. It's not right.

Regular: Call, and if they say it's okay, call back. And keep calling. Even if it takes months.

CASE STUDY: CALLS CAN WORK

Sheila owned a communications consulting company. The client—usually the chief strategist, communications VP, or COO—trusted her to solve communications problems that interfered with daily operations. She'd research the problem, develop a plan to solve it, implement the plan, and train contractors or employees to do the rest.

As you can imagine, Sheila's business was quite specialized and professional. Ads in the local newspaper were out (they wouldn't reach her large corporate customers) and ads in the *Wall Street Journal* were too expensive. So she relied on calls. In fact, for years, Sheila had an employee who made the telephone marketing calls in addition to her other responsibilities. She paid the employee a small commission and a competitive salary.

In terms of success rate: Sheila's employee made approximately fifty calls a week—sometimes more, sometimes less. Of that amount, she usually got four clients a year. That's four out of hundreds. But each of those clients usually lasted five years or more, and brought in anywhere from $30,000 to $200,000 a year. With only four employees total, and little overhead, Sheila made an impressive profit.

Chapter 16

The "Who" of Instant Marketing

One of your best bets for almost free—or even totally free—marketing is other people. They come in two categories, with countless possibilities of how you can tap into their marketing potential.

Employees: Almost Free

Yes, you do have to pay your employees' salary. But you don't need a dedicated employee for every one of your marketing requirements. In fact, think of your employees as marketing associates. And consider the talents necessary for a strong marketing campaign with each person you hire. For example, are they technologically astute? If so, they can help you with the electronic aspects of your marketing: updating your website, getting your business more presence on search engines, and finding possible exposure through blogs or chat rooms.

Here's an additional list of skills you should look for in employees. No one has all of them, and these skills are second to the professional skills directly connected to your organization's reason for being, but collectively your employees should cover all bases.

Writing Skills

You do not want a person whose writing experience was within a particular industry. For example, if you happen to be in banking or technology, don't look for someone who did a stint drafting marketing materials in those kinds of businesses. Chances are his brain has clots of clichés wedged in so deeply that when he writes, that's all that comes out. Reconditioning him and getting him to embody your particular brand can be daunting feats.

Instead, go for someone with a background in journalism, magazine writing, or advertising. They usually come with ready-made writing skills and double doses of creativity. Last word: don't ask a prospective employee if they have great writing skills. No one is likely to say, "Actually no, I don't. In fact, my writing is basically abysmal."

Instead, give him a test. Have him write a paragraph that is loosely—not directly—related to your work. So, if technology is your thing, have him describe the wonders of an old-model PC, even though everyone wants the best and newest. Or have him write a description of his ideal software package. The main point: don't have him write an essay. Make it as close to the real thing as possible, given he doesn't know details about your particular brand or offering. And keep the sample to one paragraph.

Interactive Skills

The "gift of gab," as it's called, can be immensely helpful when you go to trade shows, host events, attend association meetings, and greet customers.

Introverts, smart and driven as they might be, will never achieve this, no matter how much coaxing or training you provide. So find employees with real talent for engaging others in conversation, and let them know one part of their duties will be marketing. Few people are wild about telephone marketing, but chances are your extroverts will agree to pick up the phone. As for the rest, it should prove a real plus to the job.

Research Abilities

For many businesses, customers may be elusive. You know they're out there, but they might as well be hiding beneath rocks or holed up in caves. That's especially true if you train, consult, and provide other services to businesses, especially large corporations. How do you reach the decision-makers? How do you even find their names? You need to dig. And some people love digging. Even better, they're good at it. A few quick flights into cyberspace and they'll return with more names, numbers, and web addresses than you ever imagined. In the process, you might even get some good marketing ideas.

Artistic Abilities

This can help with signs, brochures, and even your logo if you don't have one. If you're in retail, that artistic ability will prove invaluable when you go to dress up a window for the new season or stock the shelves with a little more panache.

If you have a retail operation or other service, like a bank, where you have high face-time with customers, make sure you've "brand-trained" your employees. Naturally, they already know the intricacies of your business. If you fix computers, for example, you can trust them to take apart the innards of your customer's most precious professional tool. But can you trust them to display the kind of humor, professionalism, or courtesy that reflects your brand?

Emphasize to them that it's all about your brand and how to best reflect it. There's clothing, of course. If your brand is upscale, then your employees should dress the part. If you're going for hip, then hip clothes go. Of course, you can't dictate an individual's style, but you can set a course by dressing that way yourself and making suggestions about what works best. Don't have a dress code? Now's a great time to draft one.

As far as outside training goes, consider what your employees most need to know so they're thoroughly versed in your brand. If you bill yourself as professionals, send them to conferences, seminars, and everything else to enhance their knowledge base. If you can't spend the bucks, no matter. Bring an expert in for brown-bag lunches. Or have your employees conduct monthly presentations.

If you have a suggestion box with forms, make sure your questions get the responses critical to your brand. Rather than simply saying, "Was the service friendly?" try something more exact, like "Do our employees thoroughly address your questions?" This will help you give employees more specific constructive feedback.

Partnerships: Totally Free

Partnerships are everything in business. They can quadruple one marketing effort, and build relationships that give and give. There are a few things to remember about your partnerships. First, they need to be win-win. Whatever you get from your partner, you need something to give in return.

What you're returning is entirely in the eyes of the beholder, though. Take John Baumgartner, owner of Elegance, an illustrious "Furniture, Lighting, Accessories" store. John is a marketing whiz, finding opportunities in hidden places. Look at the neighboring clothing store window, and what do you see? Gorgeous clothing elegantly draped over furniture so beautiful you want to lounge in it for hours. Go to the local garden tour, where well-coiffed women take a peek in backyard gardens, and what do you see on the patio of the most impressive one? Furniture with Elegance tags.

Obviously, the deal gets John great exposure. But what does it get the clothing store owner? Or the folks who own the garden? They get gorgeous and altogether untouched props for free that make them look that much better. Other times, the deal sweetener is financial. No, you do not want to pay your partner for marketing your goods. Then you have a business deal and not a free marketing effort. But you can split the cost of advertising or mailers.

For example, Tony's Bistro and Limousine, Inc., concocted a great deal where customers get picked up by a limousine, go to Tony's for some fine Italian cuisine with all the trimmings, and leave in the waiting limo. The two companies offered the deal together, split the cost of advertising it, and drove all the way to the bank afterward. They also chose their timing carefully: spring, with all the weddings and proms, was prime, as was New Year's Eve.

This leads to the second point: make sure your partner is in a complementary, but not competitive, area. For example, WeMow Landscaping advertises their landscaping and pond services at Potomac Nurseries. While the nursery carries everything from mulch to trowels, once you buy the goods, it's your problem. Thanks to WeMow Landscaping, the nursery can satisfy their customers' requests for help once the pea pebbles are piled in their yards. Even better, WeMow Landscaping buys their supplies from you-know-who.

Make sure the partnership requires little or no added effort. You're not trying to market someone else; you're trying to maximize your own marketing efforts. Do favors, shell out more than your share of the bucks, and the benefits will disintegrate even before the first customers start coming in.

Here are a few more partnership ideas:

Paper Trails

This is where you exhibit, mail, or otherwise share your paper materials with your partner's clients. Are your partners sending a mailing? See if you can add in one of your direct mail pieces. Do they have an ad in the newspaper? Perhaps you can advertise with them.

Naturally, leave your brochures, flyers, business cards, and other marketing materials at your partner's business. They will provide useful services for their customers and bring plenty of business to you. Also, think creatively. One woman I know owns a housekeeping service. She partnered with a realtor who left her housekeeping brochures in the empty houses and in his office. First thing the new owners did? Called her to send a team in for a top-to-bottom scrubbing.

Block Parties

Here's a tip if your business resides in a cluster of stores, preferably running through a small town or community neighborhood. Organize other merchants to participate in a special sale. Give it any name you want. It can be your typical Spring Sale, or give it a name like the Winter Rush 20 Percent Off Sale. In nice weather, you can put your offerings outside; in cold weather, you can put a sign outside your doors and in your window announcing: "We participate in the Winter Rush." Or you could even have a design (a snowflake or large "20%") that indicates they participate.

Naturally, you'll pool money for ads, share responsibility for news releases, and combine offerings. By the way, if you provide a service, whether you're a mechanic, CPA, attorney, or physician, you can participate, too! Hand out those tip sheets and giveaways and offer a related freebie like 20 percent off your first tax consultation or a free blood pressure test.

Team Teaching

In the next section of this book, we'll look at options you have to position yourself as the expert. Chief among them: leading seminars at your client's site, at your workplace, in adult education centers, and at conferences. But you don't have to go it alone. You can conduct these seminars with a partner who will add to your knowledge base, conduct complementary breakout sessions, and put steam into your presentation.

When choosing your partner, find someone with a complementary style. If you're an introvert, find an extrovert. You can play the straight guy and your partner can ad-lib and tell jokes in between the serious information-giving. Or if you have a great sense of humor, find a second funny guy: you can bounce off each other's humor, give helpful information, and win over any crowd.

Co-Sales

Say you own a car wash. Contact the guy down the block who owns a car dealership and see about striking a deal. You give a discount for, say, six car washes to anyone who purchases a car from their lot. Your partner gives customers an added bonus to sweeten the deal. Or seek out programs run by your local community. For example, Washington, D.C., hosts a program where numerous high-end restaurants offer fabulous discounts on their lunches and dinners for a finite amount of time. The *Washington Post* carries ads publicizing the event, and local business owners, government workers, and students seize the chance to try new places. Think they return the rest of the year? You better believe it.

Chapter 17

Roadside Marketing: Lobbies, Windows, and Signs

There's no marketing more instant than your roadside appeal. That means anything the passersby see as they happen to be driving or strolling or biking down the road. As for price, your roadside appeal can be closer to almost free than you think. Unusual possibilities abound, but creativity is required!

Signs

On the Small Business Association's website (www.sba.gov), they have a saying: "A business without a sign is a sign of no business." Of course, you could also say, "A business with a good sign is a sign of good business, and a business with a bad sign is a sign of no business." That's because, of everything on your roadside marketing list, signs say the most the fastest. Make it interesting, and your customer is interested. Make it compelling, your customer is compelled. But above all, make it visible!

How you achieve visibility isn't a matter of rocket science, but it does require planning and awareness of local requirements. Most communities limit the size and placement of signs, so your first step should be to find out about these restrictions. Then make sure your sign has these qualities:

• **Clear lettering that's easy for the customer to read.** The font and other design aspects of the lettering, such as thickness or size, should depend on your brand. If you go to a professional sign maker, make sure you review the design with that in mind.

• **An appealing image.** This should be your logo. They see it on T-shirts, bumper stickers, advertisements, bags, and your sign, and love at fifth sight kicks in. Or, if they're new to town and see a really appealing sign, love at *first* sight kicks in and they walk through your door.

• **Minimal wording.** Try to stick to five or six words, tops. That means the name of your business and a little bit about it. So for example, you could say:

Sumptuous Sweets

Baked Goods, Handmade Candies

Or simply:

Featherweight

Recording Studio

with the logo of a feather in the background.

If you offer a service—whether you're an attorney, psychologist, consultant, or veterinarian—make sure you place your phone number and/or website address on your sign. You can't expect to get much walk-in traffic, but you don't want to miss any chances:

Chauncey & Stevens

Attorneys-at-Law

Personal Injury

(304) 555-1256

• **Visibility.** You want your sign to be as large as possible, simply because larger signs are easier to see. How large? As I mentioned, that depends on the restrictions of your community. Go for the biggest you can. Also, consider the options for lighting. Signs market for you 24/7, so you want them visible at night. Flashing neon might work, depending on your neighbors. If not, think about tasteful alternatives that you, and your community, can live with.

• **Color.** Naturally, you want a color that customers can see, but stay within your brand. If you're a psychologist, better not go for neon red. But if you own a day care center, hot pinks, greens, and yellows will fit in perfectly. Also, consider the color of your building. Even if you didn't— or can't—choose the shade, you need your sign to complement whatever's there.

• **Professional finish.** Unless you're a pro, don't go it alone. Hire a sign painter. The costs vary greatly, but trust me, it's worth it. Of course, you could lease a sign, but then you must make regular monthly payments. With cash flow as a major issue for small businesses, don't rent.

By the way, you can list your sign as one of your expenses when you go for a business loan. Check with your bank or the Small Business Association for more.

Generally, getting your sign made requires a three-step process. You create a rough draft of the sign, including the logo and whatever words you want to put on it. Or head for your nearest sign maker, which will have options for you to select, including shapes, colors, and designs. But remember, keep *your* brand in mind through the whole thing. Next, the sign maker creates a draft of your sign. These days, most sign makers are computerized in some way, so the draft can be played with pretty easily. Once you approve it, they make the real thing.

Usually, sign makers want money down, so be prepared. And signs take from one to two months to prepare—or longer, depending on the sign and the season. Don't have time to go in? You can also order signs online.

QUICK Tip

Get Feedback: Experiment with your sign to find what works best. Take the draft of your sign and ask passersby to look at it for a second or two (literally) then tell you what they remember. Maybe use two different designs, then survey people to determine which works better.

Window Displays

If your window displays work right, then window-shopping becomes obsolete because the customer will walk through the door and shop inside. So, consider your display a tempting taste for customers of what's inside. You want to lure them in by piquing their curiosity and making promises that, once they walk through the door, you keep.

Even better, window displays are free or almost free depending on how you want to create them. You can hire someone to design your window for you. The price can go as low as $100 a shot, especially if you're willing to barter. If you decide to design the window yourself, all the better, but make sure you get plenty of feedback, especially after your first few tries.

Either way, you'll need to change your display frequently—every month or two. Let it drag on for too long and most people stop looking. Besides, the display gradually acquires a dusty, dingy appearance. You wouldn't hand out a grease-stained or wrinkled brochure, right? Same idea for your window.

So, how do you maintain an attractive and professional look to your window—for almost nothing? Use your existing merchandise and props that you pick up just about anywhere: Goodwill, Wal-Mart, yard sales, your grandmother's attic. Most likely, some of the props will be seasonal, such as Halloween or Christmas displays, so reserve a prop room where they'll stay safe and dry for the following year. Or mix and match your elements: your Christmas lights can serve as the backdrop for a festive summer display. Here are some other tips:

• **Think lighting.** Make sure your lighting is good, playing up the most interesting aspects of your display without leaving anything in the dark. Spotlights can do wonders, although floor lights can work, too, depending on your window.

• **Use your ups and downs.** Nothing's as uninspiring as a window display with a few items hovering on the ledge. Try giving your display dimension. Use fishing wire to hang objects from the top, and use lifts at the bottom, such as furniture, boxes draped with cloth, or interesting stacks. For example, shoe stores can get a great look by stacking shoe boxes. If you own a hardware company, think about the possibilities, from buckets to stepladders to shovels.

• **Add backdrops.** These can be anything from fabric to a poster suspended from fishing wire. The backdrops add dimension and help your customer's eye focus where you want it to go.

• **Pique with promises.** A sign of some sort is always helpful. Keep it fresh, make it exciting, and make it limited. Sales work wonders, whether "50% Off Selected Merchandise!" or a holiday special. Or announce something new, imported, or somehow special: "NEW! From Iceland. 100% Pure Wool Blankets" works better than "Wool Blankets Inside." But don't keep it up there too long—after a week or two the power diminishes.

• **Keep it clean and tidy.** It doesn't matter if you're selling inner tubes—the look of your display reflects the quality of your merchandise. Greasy, messy, or otherwise dubious window displays equal dubious merchandise in your customer's mind.

QUICK Tip

Shop Around: Go to trade shows (gift shows, flower and garden shows, special retail exhibits) for more ideas. You'll get some great ideas to tweak your creativity even if you sell something as straightforward as computers or Harley Davidsons. And yes, you can take pictures for reference later.

CASE STUDY: AND THE WORST WINDOW DISPLAY AWARD GOES TO . . .

This one goes to a Thai restaurant I know—and there are so many like it—that decorates its window with plastic plants covered with a thick layer of dust. To add insult to injury, it also has the live variety, teetering on death, with yellow leaves that trigger nasty thoughts about what might be secretly mingling with the Pad Thai noodles.

Love That Lobby

Your lobby, the interior of your showroom, or your shop can make a powerful marketing statement. The lobby ranks as one of the biggest marketing investments for banks. For professionals, the lobby creates a state of mind that could shape the customer's experience of the whole visit.

To get the most marketing muscle from your lobby, you need to address how it affects *all* the senses, not just how it looks. Here's what you should consider:

The Look

What your customers see the moment they walk in the door is the most demanding requirement of your lobby. Naturally, you want the furniture to look nice and professional. But ask yourself what purpose you want the furniture to serve. If you own property, and the lobby is a walk-through area where your residents and their guests hurry through, you may want the furniture to look ornamental. A beautiful nineteenth-century antique chair might work nicely (provided you have a doorman to guard it), especially if you want an upscale look.

If you expect people to wait, then opt for more comfortable furnishings. Beanbag chairs are definitely out, unless you're trying for a hip image that reaches the younger (and more flexible) crowd. If your lobby happens to be in a bank, CPA firm, or other conservative enterprise, you may feel inclined to place the comfortable chairs near your account managers.

Maybe you want customers to stay a while, especially on a cold or rainy day so they can warm up. This serves numerous advantages: your employees can chat with them—and seal their loyalty—and customers walking in will see a full and happy house. Most places put out magazines, and some offer coffee, tea, water, and hot chocolate that the customers can help themselves to. We'll talk more about the wonders of coffee in a minute.

Regardless, make sure your furniture establishes your brand, matching your overall image and color scheme.

While you're at it, make your lobby useful. Put out those tip sheets we discussed earlier. Customers will probably read them while waiting; even better, they'll take them home. Have a container with your give-aways in it, such as packaged candies with your logos all over them. Some places have televisions running all the time. This can forge a professional, newsy type of feel to your lobby, particularly if you're in finance, PR, or security, although you want the sound down to a drone or muted altogether. Obviously, this isn't *Desperate Housewives* we're talking about, but CNN or CNBC can work nicely.

Perhaps one of the most critical—and often overlooked—aspects of a lobby is the color. Go for softer hues and comfortable lighting. Fluorescent is definitely out. It gives faces a sickly greenish hue, a particular liability if you run a dentist's office or health clinic. On the showroom floor, place the spotlight on particular products, and be sure to illuminate those display racks tucked in a corner.

Then there are your employees. The moment a customer walks into your lobby, someone should greet him—a warm, friendly greeting. If he needs to wait, offer him a drink. You might be in the mood to serve whiskey, but alas, in most establishments, the drinking is restricted to coffee, water, or tea. Still, having a drink will give your customer something to do as he waits and builds a rapport with you. If the customer winds up waiting longer than five minutes, have your receptionist put in a follow-up call, report back to the customer, and apologize, if appropriate.

The Smell

Freud said that in memory, our sense of smell is strongest. I don't know if that's true, but smell sure plays a major role in creating an impression that's powerful yet subtle. How your lobby smells can influence your customer's first impression and support or undermine your brand. For example, most realtors infuse the homes they show with the scent of fresh-baked cookies. This helps interested buyers subconsciously place the home in context of a happy, warm, and loving life.

The smell of your lobby obviously depends on your business. Candles can add a relaxed feel to an upscale retail store while incense can enhance the smell of everything from the front hall of a restaurant to a gym.

Try to think out of the box, too. A moment ago, I mentioned the value of serving your customers coffee or having a supply out and ready for them. Coffee serves another purpose, too. The lingering smell helps create a friendly atmosphere in lobbies people usually equate with cold, all-business environments like banks. If your business is located in a high-rise or sterile kind of building, and you want more of an earthy feel, try a light touch of patchouli. Really light—you don't want your older customers to have flashbacks of hippie dens.

The Sound

You probably know the value of music in restaurants and elevators. But consider the sounds that welcome your customers into your office lobby as well. If you're a dentist, are they greeted with the sound of drills? If your office is on a busy street, are visitors blitzed with the sounds of horns beeping and sirens whirring? Or if you're in an office complex, perhaps they hear nothing at all. Just stony silence. You need to determine the most suitable sounds for your office, from having a soundproof lobby or conference room where you meet and greet customers to the distant—yet distinct—hum of jazz.

The Feel

Are your doors easy to open? Is the furniture comfortable? How about temperature? All these factors can influence how your customers feel when they step inside your lobby. If you own a movie theater, hotel, or nightclub where customers might wait in lines outside, be sure to have an outdoor heating system. While it might cost more than sidewalk space or an awning, the investment will go a long way toward keeping your customers happy.

The Taste

We're talking coffee again, and any giveaway treats you might have in the office, such as mints and lollipops for the kids. Lots of businesses, like the Business Bank we mentioned earlier, are having great luck hosting brunches and other food-enhanced festivities for by-invitation customers and their referrals. The better the food the better their taste for you.

Other Considerations with Your Lobby

Do you have one entrance or two? If delivery people are coming in and out all day, they may distract the customer and create the wrong impression. If you have a showroom of some sort and a workspace out back, do you really want your employees walking through the nice front rooms in dusty jeans? In that case, consider having a separate entrance for employees out back.

Also, don't forget about suggestion boxes. These do more than offer you the chance to hear from your customers. They can also serve these purposes:

• Give you the opportunity to get feedback on specific aspects of your business. Trying a new system? Made changes to your menu? Ask about these at your suggestion box or on cards at the tables or workstations. Remember, the more specific your questions the more specific the answers you'll receive.

• Get names and numbers. Have your customers write their vital information, such as phone numbers, email addresses, and mailing addresses on the back of their cards. They'll go straight into your mailing list. If someone says something especially constructive, negative, or positive, you might want to email them a response.

• Show you really do care about your customers. Everyone says it, but you prove it here.

Be sure that your suggestion box is clean, professional, and prominently displayed. A dusty box wedged into a corner is your quintessential anti-marketing message.

CASE STUDY: AND THE COOLEST LOBBY IDEA IN CREATION AWARD GOES TO . . .

The Heart Clinic in Rancho Mirage, California, installed a giant, walk-through heart in their lobby, turning an ordinary entryway into a museum. As they walk through, visitors learn how their heart works and pick up nuggets of healthy-heart information. The lobby attracts hundreds of visitors each week, including school groups and tourists, and it serves a double purpose by providing a public service to its visitors and making more people aware of the facility.

According to Adam Rubinstein, who helped design and implement the fixture, just about any business can have a museum in its lobby. Own a skateboard or bicycle shop? Turn a back room into a history lesson, showing pictures or the real thing, from the earliest models to the present. You can display photos and blurbs about all-star riders and promote your offerings at the same time.

Have a coffee shop? Try turning part of your wall space into a display of how the beans are grown and harvested. While you're at it, think about selling books on the subject or bundling the books with one of your mugs (with your logo on it), a bag of your coffee (with your logo, again!), and even a coffee accessory, if you happen to sell them.

If you do it right, the museum will be a draw for customers. Once they're in, they'll want to stay.

CASE STUDY: AND THE SECOND COOLEST LOBBY AWARD GOES TO . . .

Dr. Perez, the Kids' Dentist, has got the lobby idea nailed. Walk in the door and you feel like you've entered the year 2020, with game stations built into the wall like something from NASA, a small movie screen facing the chair of every patient, and a very futuristic feel. The brand convinces parents that the doctor is one step ahead when it comes to dentistry, and the kids think this place, the *dentist's* office, is cooler than cool. It's amazing: kids actually rush in, heading straight for the games, and parents have to pull them out when it's time to leave.

QUICK Tip

Lobbies Out of the Box: Here's an amazing lobby idea, also from Adam Rubinstein: read through theme- and amusement-park magazines. These guys are experts at establishing the look and feel of a place, and you could get plenty of ideas from them. Or on your next trip to Disneyland with the kids, take a notebook and camera, but not just to photograph the rides. Take pictures of the interesting images that surround you and observe how they use light and dimension to get special effects.

Adam also recommends a sense of artistry and play. Think about using odd angles and shapes, like twisted windows, off-center tables, animated objects, and flashing designs on your walls. You can also play around with your lobby so that it reflects your brand and even your occupation. If you own a sporting goods manufacturing plant, you can have balls suspended at odd angles from the walls and ceiling. Be creative, even if you feel your occupation says otherwise.

For example, if you're a CPA, think about having big numbers decorating your walls. Facilities specializing in some aspect of plumbing have a literally golden opportunity to have a giant plumbing fixture suspended on the lobby walls or exposed pipes (dressed for showing) above the room. Own a plant that manufactures airplane parts? Have a plane, or a less expensive replica, hanging at an angle from the ceiling. An airplane museum might be a good idea, too. Can't afford the real thing? Think about pictures.

Outside Extras

Virtually every aspect of your business lends itself to roadside marketing, not just the ones we've addressed so far. Think about the building where you house your business. It offers enormous marketing opportunities. If you're old enough, you may remember the White Castle restaurants that looked like white castles.

Granted, some building ideas are a lot more expensive than others. And most small businesses simply don't have the wherewithal to invest in this more extreme form of marketing. You could consider lower-priced alternatives, though. For example, the bar Madam's Organ, based in the funky Adam's Morgan area of Washington, D.C., boasts live music, southern cooking, and plenty to drink. The inviting front porch on the exterior, while on a bustling multicultural street, makes the place look as though it could be in the heart of old New Orleans.

The owners of Madam's Organ went one step further. They painted a sassy (and deliciously controversial) mural on one wall of their building. It's of a bosomy, albeit fictionalized, Madam. The mural itself is a part of D.C. history. It lures tourists, students, and neighborhood regulars inside, and thanks to the controversy surrounding it, has a notoriety advertisers could only pray for.

If you decide on murals, or any other major ventures, be my guest. Trust me, they work. But better check your community codes first, especially if you live in a historic location. Some of these historic—or otherwise conservative—neighborhoods restrict any superfluous outdoor painting, even something as simple as your name on the mailbox. Some districts may even stipulate the number of stories or style of the buildings.

Don't forget banners. They're particularly good for announcing a sale or special offer that your competitors don't have. Are you located on a strip clustered with similar businesses? Do you own an auto dealership? Bank? Restaurant? Clothing store? A banner could be the pivotal point between having customers entering your door or someone else's. If you go down the banner road, remember to keep it simple. One logo. One message. Three or four words. And keep it big. Your customers must see it, even if they're driving past at sixty miles an hour.

If you need to go altogether free, not to worry. There's still plenty you can do. If you're in retail, display a sample of your offerings on the sidewalk. Or have a "25% OFF" rack. Customers will notice the rack through your window and come on in. If they decide to buy one of the bargain items, even better. They'll still have to come in and pay, and look at the other merchandise when they do.

Another great marketing possibility: lines. Yes, you do want lines, especially if you own a restaurant or theater. This shows the world how popular your business really is and catches the attention of passersby. Of course, the lines must come to you, and you certainly don't want to make a point of forcing people to wait. But if they're there, and if you know other customers will see them, make them happy. If it's cold, have overhead heaters. And have a canopy in case of rain.

Finally, be creative. Cracker Barrel made a megamillion-dollar business by having people wait on their rocking chairs (for sale), where they play checkers on big checkerboards (also for sale), and stroll through their waiting area exhibiting old-fashioned goods (most definitely for sale). And do people buy? Have you ever been to a Cracker Barrel? Didn't you? If you own a theater, how about having an employee sell peanuts, candy, and popcorn to people while they wait? The possibilities are endless—and free. If they don't pay off, you didn't lose anything by trying and can move on to your next marketing venture.

Chapter 18

The People in the Places: Marketing Face-to-Face

Networking is a well-known marketing strategy; some think it's *the* marketing strategy. But what happens if you aren't in a network, or want to expand the network you already have? The answer: join an association. You may have noticed in this book that there's a mind-boggling number of associations. Not wimpy little groups in someone's basement, but big, well-funded societies that have chapters everywhere. There's an association for advertisers, for radio advertisers, for radio makers. It's amazing.

Generally, most associations give you what marketers crave most: exposure. They usually hold monthly breakfast meetings and other get-togethers where you give your one-minute spiel and, once a year, a longer presentation. This will give you the opportunity to network, get new clients, and, even better, get valuable information from peers. There are three types of associations to choose from. Let's take a look at them, and then talk a little about the pros, cons, and secrets to getting the most from them.

• **Chamber of Commerce and other state or locally sponsored groups.** They'll supply you with ample information about community events, loan opportunities, and more. Even better, you'll meet other small-business people who can share their marketing experience, loop you into their networks, and even purchase your services. So, the Chamber of Commerce is especially good for start-up businesses.

• **Industry-related organizations.** You'll meet people in your line of work. You can share experience, learn new strategies, and compare clients. Depending on the association, you can also attend national conferences with guest speakers, activities, and booths where you can peruse useful products and services and display your own. We'll talk about booths later.

• **Specialty organizations like the Professional Business Women's Association (PBWA).** This group has one hundred or so members, most in the forty-to-fifty age range. Since they've typically owned their businesses for some time, most join to socialize, compare notes, and generally have a good time. These smaller groups are great rallying points for support and feedback, although you probably won't generate a lot of business from attending the meetings.

Pros: As you probably guessed, the real pro is the people you meet and the relationships you cultivate. You can also get a heads-up on what's new and best in your industry so you have an edge in your marketing and just about everything else.

Cons: Most associations charge money to join. They usually have a sliding scale of sorts, charging one- or two-person operations a smaller amount than, say, a large corporation. The fees can range from under $100 (think small and local) to $1,000 and up. Still, money is money and you may not want to pay.

Then there's that second expense: your time. The central aspect of joining an association is meeting people and sealing those relationships. Repeat performances on your part are a must. You can always send employees, of course, but their time is your money, and the results simply won't be the same.

Secrets: Think about joining an organization that's slightly different from what you do, although not exceptionally so. For example, if you have a housecleaning business, think about joining an association of realtors. They'll be the first to know about homes that are being bought and sold, and which require industrial-strength cleaning. If you're a voice coach, try joining a speakers' association. They'd love to have you conduct helpful seminars and publicize your offerings.

QUICK Tip

Find the Best Groups for You: Make a list of three associations you might like to join. Then do the following:

• Call one or two members to learn more

• Attend one of their meetings as a guest

• Look at their monthly and annual schedules

Then, with that information in hand, ask yourself these questions:

• What do I want to get from the association? Contact with peers who can help build my marketing techniques? Actual clients? Will the association give me these opportunities?

• Do the scheduled events match my schedule? (If you need to be at work before sunrise, breakfast meetings probably won't work for you.)

• Does the culture of the organization match my personality and brand? (If you own a car dealership and are marketing high-end cars, you probably won't want to join a group like PBWA. These women probably want to invest in retirement, not BMWs.)

Of course, you may know about an association that just knocks your socks off, but for no good reason. Want to join? Why not? Go ahead.

Adult Education Courses

Adult education centers are a great place to learn. They're also a great place to teach and market your products or services. While they may not pay a lot, they give you the best kind of exposure possible: a group of people who are interested in what you do and are willing to pay for more. Even better, they give you the chance to create personal relationships with prospective customers with more marketing impact than any ad, phone call, or direct mail piece.

Many years ago, when I was starting my consulting service, I taught classes at the Boston Center for Adult Education (BCAE). Housed in a beautiful former mansion in Boston's Back Bay, it attracted professionals from all over the city. My classes ranged from a three-hour editing course to an eight-week writing class that met one evening a week. Those classes launched my career.

It usually worked this way: my students became my private clients, coming to my office for hourly sessions. Many of them invited me into their workplaces, where I offered training sessions to groups, which spawned jobs writing and editing, which spawned jobs developing style guides . . . before I knew it, I had contracts of $50,000 or more a year, all thanks to the adult education class.

So, here's what you need to do.

Determine What You Have to Offer

Base that decision on what you think people want to learn. Say you have a legal practice. People certainly don't want to learn the intricacies of legal language. But they will want to learn their legal rights when purchasing a house or even getting a divorce.

Pick an Adult Education Center

If you live in a city, you may have several adult education centers to choose from. My advice is to pick just one for a start; you don't want to spread yourself too thin. Your biggest consideration is the kind of adults these places attract. When I taught years ago, I had several choices. One, as you know, was the BCAE. But Cambridge, a relatively close distance from my house, also housed the Cambridge Center for Adult Education. The Cambridge Center was only a block from Harvard, a half-block from Radcliff, a few blocks from MIT, and shouting distance from countless other small colleges. So, why did I choose BCAE? Simple. Just about everyone who lived near the Cambridge Center was either a professor or a student already and didn't need to attend the program. Besides, the competition for students was intense, seeing how most of the schools offered their own evening courses where students could attend classes taught by university professors at a fraction of the daytime price. The Cambridge Center offered fewer classes and fewer students!

Don't think there's an adult education center near you? Chances are you can find something. Adult education centers are everywhere. I live in a five-hundred-person town in West Virginia. No adult education there? Guess again. I live near a small college that offers numerous programs to adults in the surrounding towns. And with so few options, they all flock there! Besides, just about every church, synagogue, and YMCA offers something, and if they don't, most would be happy to start!

Look in the Adult Education Center Brochure

This will teach you what classes are available that might be like yours. If you happen to be a lawyer and see that they already offer a class on knowing your legal rights during a divorce, don't panic. You may not be able to teach that class, but the news isn't entirely bad. It shows that a market for classes like it—and your services—exists. So, try thinking up other classes related to the subject, like "Everything you need to know about prenuptial agreements" or "Know your children's legal rights during your divorce."

Pitch Your Class

You can send the director a course description, but my advice is to call first. Talk to the director. Describe your strengths and your experience. If you haven't trained before, don't worry. Explain that you're an expert in the subject matter, that you will develop a top-notch curriculum, and that you will be happy to start with one short session to prove how successful you'll be. Once you make that personal connection, you'll be able to pitch new classes or get penciled in when another teacher leaves.

Develop a Class Description

This one- or two-paragraph piece is central to your pitch and the course description that will appear in the adult education manual. Here's what you do:

- Start the paragraph with a pithy line: "Believe it or not, divorce can be easier than you think, once you know your legal rights."
- Support the opening line: "And in this class, you'll get critical information from a top divorce attorney, including the Top Ten Divorce Mistakes You Must Avoid; case studies that show you how two really can tango, even in divorce court; and important legal dos and don'ts when working with your lawyer."
- Show what the participants will know how to do when they leave: "Among the many results, you'll develop a priority list of what to fight for and what to accept, essential steps you can take to prepare your children for the future, a road map for the fastest and most practical way to divide your property, and much more."

Market, Market, Market

Once you start teaching, send out a press release announcing the courses to local papers. And remember to put your name and web address on every page of every handout, tip sheet, and worksheet you give participants. This will be a subtle reminder that you're available to them whenever they're ready. And trust me, they'll be ready faster than you think.

Conferences

All sorts of organizations—from federal, state, and local governments to private companies and nonprofit associations—hold events that can attract hundreds of participants. They're often held in major cities, with plenty of hotel space and conference centers the size of football stadiums, but they also crop up in towns, small cities, everywhere—even church basements.

These events take place virtually year-round, but especially at peak times: January, February, March, April, May, September, and October. And they offer you two great marketing opportunities—speaking engagements and booth space—often at reasonable prices. In fact, sometimes there's no cost except your personal expenses. Sometimes you can even get paid to attend. Let's explore these opportunities in more detail.

Speaking Engagements

So why speak at a conference? For the same reason you should teach an adult education class: exposure where you are neatly positioned as an expert. But getting those coveted speaker slots can be difficult. If you haven't delivered talks or training before, start with smaller events, like those hosted by your local Chamber of Commerce, and work yourself into the bigger venues.

Start small, in front of a familiar, and hopefully local, audience. You may not have a choice in that regard, since most associations want experienced speakers only. You'll have to write a proposal, of course, which will include the bio you developed in the first section of this book; handouts, which could include your tip sheets; and a description of your presentation. These sessions can last anywhere from ninety minutes to a full day; it's your choice. You could also win the coveted keynote speaker spot, but my advice: if you haven't already been a speaker, don't even try. Work your way into it. You can't undo a bad presentation.

Here are some pointers:

• Pick a topic that will give the participants information they can immediately use.

• Case studies are all the rage these days, so you need to use lots of examples, with plenty of outcomes attached.

• Sure, use PowerPoint if you must—people use it all the time. But limit yourself to three or four bullets per slide and cut the clutter. PowerPoint does have its downside, as I mentioned earlier. Most PowerPoint presentations aren't especially interesting, and the participants end up looking at the slides and not you.

• Use humor. People love humor. Open with humor and keep the humor going all through the talk. If humor isn't your thing, tell stories. Improvise. Give fascinating tidbits of information, using surprising statistics, interesting connections to historical events, and quotes the participants will remember. And above all, make sure they stay awake.

• Give tip sheets and handouts. And guess what should go at the bottom of each one? And at the top? And anywhere else where it tastefully fits? That's right: your logo, website, and phone number.

Try not to get too technical. People come and go in these things, and unless you're at an academic conference, they generally want quick hits of information that will immediately improve their lives.

Trade Show Booths

Just about every city, large and small, hosts trade shows. You'd be amazed at the number and variety of people who attend. As for setting up a company booth, no question you'll walk out with leads galore, probably hundreds of them. And you'll get important exposure to everyone from suppliers to partners to customers. Giving a talk? Your appeal, and credibility as a vendor, will quadruple. Also important, you get to meet your competitors. Yes, this is where you can really scope out how the other guy prices, positions, and pitches his product and get a better idea of how to competitively position yours. And if all goes according to plan, you pluck away a few customers of your own.

But there is a downside. Free or almost free? Nope. Booths cost anywhere from hundreds to thousands of dollars, and there's no guarantee you'll actually get business. And if you participate, you have to do it right. Which means no handmade signs, display boards, or homemade giveaways. You'll be competing with countless others, and quality counts; your customer will probably have seen some variation of your offering a few dozen times already that day.

Think You Want a Booth?

The Top Twelve Must-Do List

If you want a booth, here are twelve things for your must-do list.

1. Go to the show before you actually participate in it.

Every trade show has its own personality. So go to the one you're thinking of joining and look with a critical eye. Who attends? Are people actively interacting? Attending exhibits or talks? How large is the crowd? And how does your offering fit in with the scheme? Then determine if you really want to go and if it's the best fit for your company.

2. Determine your goals.

Decide what you want from the trade show. To get leads? To make sales right then and there? To launch a new product, new location, or new approach? If you're branding yourself as an expert, how will you gauge your success? Make these goals concrete and as numerical as possible. How many leads is enough? How many sales do you hope to achieve at the show, or in the year or so after, to have made the trip worthwhile?

While this requires some guesswork, setting these goals will help you determine whether you should return the following year and what steps you can take to make the experience more lucrative next year.

3. Map your budget.

How much money are you willing to spend on the event? Itemize carefully, staying as close to free as possible. Do you need to spend a night or two in a hotel? How about your employees? How much do you want to spend on your displays? Your materials? And the all-important giveaways? Make sure you have prepared the financial end of this commitment before moving forward.

4. Book your booth.

Depending on your business, you may need to apply to the trade show, especially if you're a jeweler or craftsperson. In this case, you'll probably need to send photos of your work to the trade show selection committee. If you get turned down, don't panic. Find out why. Maybe the photos weren't strong enough or the committee already had too many exhibitors in your category. Then go to the show, learn how to do better, and try again next year.

With or without the application process, you need to book your booth. But don't simply book it. Plan it. You don't want your booth to get shoved in a corner where no one but the delivery people will see it, but you don't want to sacrifice this year's entire profit for a prime spot. So negotiate. You may be able to get more space for less money in a less impressive spot, or you may be willing to pay a premium for a wedge in a crowded spot on the floor. If it's cozy and not cramped, it might work.

5. Design your display.

You may provide more services than Wal-Mart has items, but the customer will only be able to focus on one of them. So determine the best one given the competition and your primary customer at this event. Then, plan for the booth itself, especially the all-important display. Keep it neat, with your offerings at eye-level. Apply the ideas we discussed regarding your window display and lobby: use odd angles, interesting shapes and colors, and watch the lighting. Make sure you use the right tones to play up your offering and play down the inevitable flat light of the conference center. Above all, take chances. Make sure your booth distinguishes you from all the others—meaning, of course, that you're infinitely better.

6. Add an interactive element to engage customers.

Try to think of yourself as a bug zapper, but in the most positive sense. You need to lure your customer to your booth with some sort of interactive feature. If you happen to be a health care specialist, you can offer a free blood pressure test, or maybe a quiz so participants can learn how well they're actually eating. Or think about showing a short but fascinating video or demonstrating how to use an object or procedure. Try to access as many senses as possible: have a bright, compelling visual; perhaps a treat of some sort (most exhibitors are big into bowls of candy); and music or another sound that's soft enough to be suggestive but loud enough to be heard above the trade show din.

7. Figure out interesting lead-generating devices.

Just about every vendor has a fishbowl of some sort. You drop in your card and they have a raffle later with some sort of enticing prize. Or you sign up for their newsletter and get a discount or something for free. If you need to rely on these options, go ahead. If you can find something more interesting and unique, all the better.

8. Give trade show discounts.

Trade show discounts do get people to buy—and buy quickly. Besides, most customers who show up expect some discount on their purchase. Use your discounts as a great way to get people to seek out your booth. Mention your discounts in your ads, your news release, and your website.

If you have a local crowd coming, think about giving them trade show coupons they can use for a finite time afterwards. This will encourage them to come to your business and purchase additional items while they're there.

9. Publicize, publicize, publicize.

Before the trade show, let everyone—customers, suppliers, contacts—know you're going. Advertise in your newspaper. Put it in your newsletter. And definitely put it on the Web. If you want to send out a press release, find something newsy about it. For example, if you have a new product to launch, that's the place to do it. Or if you've created an interesting package, unveil it then. Don't forget to include your booth number so customers know where to find you. Most conference spaces are big!

10. Be ready to close.

If you're planning to sell, be prepared with cash, a credit card processor, and receipts. Make sure your bags have your logo and business information, and throw in a giveaway that you know customers are going to use. Make sure you have enough people to work at the booth so as one person finalizes the transaction another can be greeting customers.

11. Practice "booth etiquette" on and off the floor.

Make sure you or your employees greet everyone who approaches your booth immediately. Offer them something, like candy or a giveaway. If possible, strike up a conversation. You and whoever is manning your booth may get burnt out from so many handshakes and so many faces, so give yourself plenty of breaks. You want to appear fresh and happy to see whoever approaches your booth.

12. Practice the persistent art of follow-up.

Once the trade show ends, your marketing begins. Make sure you follow up within a week after the show. Call. Send direct mail pieces and announcements. Get your newsletter out. If you can find a way to sweeten the deal, do so. Planning a trip? See if you can stop by their business while you're in town. Then continue following up for months ahead. Obviously, don't become a stalker, but do give them a nudge once a month or so with an interesting tip sheet, e-newsletter, or some other item that they'll value.

Show up everywhere

Consider having a booth at your local street fairs, 4-H fairs, and other events. The price is usually right, anywhere from $100 a day to free. If you're a professional service provider—such as a physician, counselor, or attorney—you may dismiss these venues as being for craft people. And in some cases, they are. But don't rule them out entirely. Set up a table with a bowl of giveaways—Hershey's Kisses work wonders—and a brochure with important tips that directly relate to the client. If you're a counselor, how about tips for lowering stress or for better change management? Visitors will save the brochure and remember you when they need help.

QUICK Tip

Build It and They Will Come: Holding seminars in your office can be tricky. Sure, people want to come, but often something prevents them. Depending on your business, you can convince customers to show up for other kinds of sessions. Lowe's, for example, has a once-a-month workshop where kids and their parents can build birdhouses, toolboxes, and other items. The materials are free and the kids bring home a reminder of their visit. As for their parents? They pick up something while they're there, and in the weeks to come they'll drive past Home Depot in order to buy that must-have item at Lowe's.

Appendix A

Worksheets

Worksheet 1

Defining Your Business

1. What is your primary product or service?_____

2. What are one or two secondary offerings you will probably add to your marketing campaign now or later?_____

3. Who is your primary customer? _____
   Who is your secondary customer?_____
   What do these customers have in common?_____

4. Who are your direct competitors?_____
   Who are your indirect competitors?_____

5. What distinguishes you from your competitors?_____

6. To what extent does your marketing rely on you?
   High___ Medium___ Low___

7. Do you have any special talents that could give you a marketing edge?
   _____

8. List ten adjectives that best describe your business:

   1. _____
   2. _____
   3. _____
   4. _____
   5. _____
   6. _____
   7. _____
   8. _____
   9. _____
   10. _____

Now, cut five that are redundant or low on your list, and keep the remaining five.

1. _____
2. _____
3. _____
4. _____
5. _____

9. List ten adjectives that your customers would use to describe your business:

1. _____   6. _____
2. _____   7. _____
3. _____   8. _____
4. _____   9. _____
5. _____   10. _____

10. What do your customers want? _____

Worksheet 2

Love You, Love Your Brand

1. List three or more products or services that you will need to name at some point. This could be a new product, a sale, or an event. Then, play around with the names. Remember those adjectives you listed in the previous chapter? Make sure the names incorporate those ideas. For example, if you own a restaurant and "healthy" is one of your adjectives, you wouldn't want to name your lunchtime special "Eat n' Run." Also, consider what your primary customer would appreciate. The result may be something like: "Fast & Fit Lunch Specials."

Offering   Name

_____   _____

_____   _____

_____   _____

_____   _____

2. Pick two of the offerings you just listed and write a tagline for both. Or, if you haven't done so already, write a tag for your business. Then rewrite, rewrite, and rewrite. Get feedback when you're done.

Offering 1:
Tag ideas: _____

_____

_____

Offering 2:
Tag ideas: _____

_____

_____

3. What are some images that best reflect your company brand? List three or four here:

_____

_____

_____

_____

What images best describe your company? They can be as abstract or concrete as you like. If you think no images are necessary, write that, too.

_____

_____

_____

Now, what are some colors? And yes, black and white count. Think Gateway!

_____

Worksheet 3

Marketing Material Checklist

Use this checklist to ensure that you have met all ten of the marketing must-dos.

❏ Included a utilitarian function

❏ Used marketing smarts

❏ Focused on the customer

❏ Accentuated the customer benefits

❏ Used a catch-and-keep approach

❏ Kept the word use clear and clean

❏ Used white space wisely

❏ Applied font savvy

❏ Considered the love at fifth sight principle

❏ Avoided anything boring, especially clichés!

Worksheet 4
Your Tool Kit

What are the top five items in your tool kit? Decide which ones in the following spaces, in order of priority. In case you forget what they are, here's the list:

- Signature materials
- Brochures
- Website
- Direct mail and email
- Short stash: tip sheets, flyers, and other one-pagers
- Newsletters
- Press releases, opinion pieces, and letters to the editor
- Ads
- Giveaways

Tool Kit Priority 1

Item:_____

Amount you're willing to invest: _____

How (and when) you plan to use it: _____

_____

_____

_____

Most important steps you need to take to develop it:

1._____
2._____
3._____
4._____
5._____

Other thoughts:

_____

_____

Tool Kit Priority 2

Item: _____

Amount you're willing to invest: _____

How (and when) you plan to use it: _____

_____

_____

Most important steps you need to take to develop it:

1._____

2._____

3._____

4._____

5._____

Other thoughts:

_____

_____

Tool Kit Priority 3

Item: _____

Amount you're willing to invest: _____

How (and when) you plan to use it: _____

_____

_____

Most important steps you need to take to develop it:

1._____

2._____

3._____

4._____

5._____

Other thoughts:

_____

_____

Tool Kit Priority 4

Item: _____

Amount you're willing to invest: _____

How (and when) you plan to use it: _____

_____

_____

Most important steps you need to take to develop it:

1._____

2._____

3._____

4._____

5._____

Other thoughts:

_____

_____

Tool Kit Priority 5

Item: _____

Amount you're willing to invest: _____

How (and when) you plan to use it: _____

_____

_____

Most important steps you need to take to develop it:

1._____

2._____

3._____

4._____

5._____

Other thoughts:

_____

_____

Worksheet 5

Telephone Sales

1. Why are you calling? Write the major response you want here:

_____

_____

_____

2. Who are you calling?

Name: _____

Position: _____

Who do you expect to reach? _____

_____

3. Who is doing the calling for you? List three good people:

1._____

2._____

3._____

4. Get phone numbers and collect a database.

5. Write your script.

6. Determine instant accessibility strategies.

7. What is the prime time for calling?

8. Create a calling log.

9. Practice the savvy art of follow-up.

10. Look into other telephone marketing possibilities.

Worksheet 6

Employees

Which of the following skills do your key employees currently have that they can use to help your marketing effort?

Technical know-how
Who: _____
Projects they can work on: _____
_____

Writing skills
Who: _____
Projects they can work on: _____
_____

Interactive skills
Who: _____
Projects they can work on: _____
_____

Research abilities
Who: _____
Projects they can work on: _____
_____

Artistic abilities
Who: _____
Projects they can work on: _____
_____

Skills you should look for in new hires: _____
_____

Skills that you need from outside vendors: _____

_____

Projects they'll undertake: _____

_____

Amount you're willing to spend: _____

Worksheet 7
Partnerships

List five potential partners and the marketing projects you can collaborate on.

1.
Partner: _____

Projects: _____

Materials: _____

Expense: _____

2.
Partner: _____

Projects: _____

Materials: _____

Expense: _____

3.
Partner: _____

Projects: _____

Materials: _____

Expense: _____

4.
Partner: _____

Projects: _____

Materials: _____

Expense: _____

5.
Partner: _____

Projects: _____

Materials: _____

Expense: _____

Worksheet 8

Courses You Can Teach

1. Determine what you have to offer.

What you have to offer: _____

What people will want to learn: _____

2. Pick an adult education center.

The best adult education center near you: _____

3. Classes you can teach:

_____

_____

_____

4. Contact names of the director, curriculum manager, or other helpful people:

_____

_____

_____

_____

5. Develop a class description.

Pithy line: _____

Support the opening line: _____

Show what the participants will know how to do when they leave:

_____

_____

6. Market, market, market.

Places where you can market: _____

_____

Appendix B

Samples

Bio Samples

Individual Bios

Long Form

Susan Benjamin, a former professor, journalist, and academic advisor, has brought communications solutions to the nation for almost twenty years. Publications from the *Wall Street Journal* to the *Chicago Tribune* have featured Susan's approaches, while her opinion pieces have appeared in Knight Ridder syndicates and other publications, including *USA Today*, the *Philadelphia Inquirer*, the *New York Daily News*, and *Government Executive*. Her most recent book, *Instant Marketing for Almost Free* (Sourcebooks), won critical praise.

As a speaker, Susan has appeared on CNNfn and National Public Radio, and at numerous conferences. She has also trained over one hundred thousand federal and private-sector employees in venues including satellite broadcasts, videos, traditional in-class forums, and executive coaching sessions.

Susan's research includes assessments of organizational communication processes and focus groups, and studies on how language affects reader responsiveness. Among other results, her research helped the U.S. government overhaul their recruitment and hiring processes and the Treasury Department validate their approach to conveying regulatory requirements. Susan's articles about these findings have appeared in publications such as *Scribes Legal Journal*, *Government Executive*, and *Employment Management Today*.

As a participant in the White House initiative on plain language, Susan oversaw the revision of electronic and hard copy documents for both private and public organizations. These ranged from health plan brochures to pension benefits notices to marketing and PR materials that hundreds of thousands of Americans receive each day. Her clients include the Department of Defense, Liberty Mutual Insurance Group, the Social Security Administration, the U.S. Office of Personnel Management, and many more.

Susan studied philosophy and writing at Boston University and Bennington College. She received her master's in writing from Lesley College where she worked with C. Michael Curtis, senior editor of the *Atlantic*.

One Paragraph

Susan Benjamin, a former professor, journalist, and academic advisor, has brought communications solutions to the nation for almost twenty years. Publications from the *Wall Street Journal* to the *New York Daily News* have featured articles by and about her. Her most recent book, *Instant Marketing for Almost Free* (Sourcebooks), won critical praise. She has appeared on CNNfn and National Public Radio and has trained over one hundred thousand employees. Susan's clients range from Fortune 100s to countless small businesses worldwide. A participant in the White House initiative on plain language, Susan has conducted research and studies for the federal and private sectors on how language triggers response. Susan holds a master's degree in writing.

Short Version

Author and trainer Susan Benjamin consults on communications issues for organizations of all sizes. Her latest book is *Instant Marketing for Almost Free*.

Business Bio

Since 1989, Consultants, Inc., has helped organizations generate significant results by managing their communications. We achieve this through a comprehensive approach that includes training, copy writing and editing, and graphic design. Our clients range from giants like Brigstone International and Forbes & Sons Consulting to over fifty small businesses. Based in Denver, Colorado, Consultants, Inc., is certified as a Very Small Business (VSB) and a woman-owned business. We have won acclaim for our innovative and successful methods from the National Institute of Small Business Enterprises and the American Association of Copywriters and received the 2003 Annual Best Business Practice award in Denver.

Brochure Sample

Cover: LOGO

The National Society of Educators

Your kids are being hijacked!

Here's what you can do to stop it!

Street Address

Phone Number

Web Address

Don't Let Your Child Be Hijacked!

Every day, millions of American children are being hijacked by forces that literally shape their brains. Forces that affect their physical, social, and psychological development. Forces that will limit their ability to thrive in the future.

So who's hijacking them? The culprit may surprise you: it's the media—and here's what you need to know.

The facts:

Children spend more time staring into a TV or computer screen than any other single activity in their lives.

Experts say that passive viewing is a primary reason for child obesity.

The physical development of children's brains is actually stunted because of continuous TV viewing.

More than half of all media project violent or stress-provoking images that affect children's security and sense of well-being.

What is the solution?

You are! By getting actively involved in how your child spends his or her free time, you can help turn these startling facts around.

Need ideas? Want to help? Call the NSE at (213) 555-7689 or email us at Questions@NSE.com.

Want to help your children?

Here's what you can do:

Encourage them to read books. Even better, read books with them.

Plan outdoor activities with the whole family or your children and their friends.

Limit screen time to one hour a day.

Make sure your children are watching appropriate shows, playing non-violent games, and avoiding dangerous websites.

Enroll your child in after-school activities, including soccer leagues, chess clubs, and drama clubs.

Call out!

"The hijacking of children's minds is the single greatest threat to education. But it's never too late to turn that situation around." Dr. Edward McVain, Associate Director, Department of State Education

Bio: Founded in 1982, the not-for-profit National Society of Educators sponsors programs to help children excel in all aspects of their lives. These include support groups for parents, summer day camps, and grassroots efforts in twenty-three states to support community centers, libraries, and other organizations. Our members include researchers, teachers, community leaders, and concerned parents. We are based in Boston, Massachusetts, and have thirty-two chapters across the country.

Want to get involved? Please complete this form and mail it to us, or email us at our website, www.nationalsocietyofeducators.com. Please check the box at the bottom of this form if you care to give a donation.

Direct Mail Sample

It's Time Again
for the
Morgan and Bart Spring Fling!

Yes, Morgan and Bart, two of Williamsburg's most notorious comedy club stars, are hosting their annual spring fling. You know the drill!

What to wear: Anything springlike and outrageous. Prize goes to the most hilarious. And guys, don't dress up as girls, okay? It's old.

When to come: March 21. The show starts at 11:00 p.m. but the doors open at 8:00 p.m.

How 'bout food? How 'bout our world-famous ribs? Okay, they're not world-famous, but they're good. And check out the slaw, too.

How 'bout the show? The lineup is star-studded. We've got Billy the Zapper, Mike and Eddy, and Paula Pearlson. And, yes, two magic shows, but we won't tell you when—they'll just magically appear.

How much? Just show up, okay? And bring your credit card.

Morgan and Bart's Comedy Show
2345 12th Street, N.W.
East Central Eastham, NY
(212) 555-0987

Want to know more? Check out our site:
www.MandBClub.com

Hey! See you there!

Tip Sheets and Flyers

This one comes from a fitness center whose primary client is a corporation with offices in four states. The fitness center sets up shop in their building or a location nearby and is partially subsidized by the company. So, the mission of this tip sheet is to get employees to live healthier lives, and go to their fitness center. They used it in their newsletter, and modified it as a flyer that HR posted on bulletin boards.

Health and Fitness Reminders

Yes, exercise is pivotal to your physical and mental well-being. But with a schedule clogged with requirements, who can find the time? Here are some tips that might help:

Head for the Fitness Center, Inc., for shorter, more focused workouts. Even a 45-minute session several times a week can keep you fit. Guaranteed, there's a center on-site or close by.

Take walks during lunchtime. You may not be near an outdoor track or mountainous path, but even a half-hour hike along a sidewalk will get your heart pumping.

Take the stairs. Generally hiking up three or four flights takes only slightly longer than an elevator ride and is the perfect cardiovascular charge. Women, beware if you're wearing high heels.

Check for healthy menus when you eat out. That includes fast-food restaurants, like McDonald's and Subway, all too conveniently near the workplace.

Bring healthy snacks like carrots, nuts, or an apple, so when snack time calls, you'll head for your lunch pack and not the junk-food machine.

Newsletter Article Sample

MLK Day: *A Day On, Not A Day Off!*

On the third Monday of January, employees nationwide will commemorate Martin Luther King, Jr. Day, the newest American national holiday. Although work is closed, remember the theme of this year's holiday: *Remember! Celebrate! Act! A Day On, Not A Day Off!*

So, how is your "day off" a "day on"? You'll find answers on the government website www.mlkday.gov. It lists community events that honor Dr. King's legacy throughout the nation. For example, the District of Columbia Jewish Community Center needs volunteers to help paint classrooms and hallways in Adams Elementary School while the Denver Governor's Commission on Community Service needs help with their "A Drum Major for Peace—A Tribute of Justice" march and parade.

If you feel more inclined to stay indoors on Martin Luther King, Jr. Day, you may want to tour these websites:

www.stanford.edu You'll find the Martin Luther King, Jr. Research and Education Institution. Don't be intimidated by the name—the site contains an array of interesting and accessible educational work about Dr. King, his times, and his contribution.

www.holiday.net Interesting information here about MLK Day and other national holidays—some you never dreamed of! The site is fun and kid-friendly.

www.americanrhetoric.com You can listen to Martin Luther King, Jr.'s "I Have a Dream" speech on this wonderful site, accompanied by text and stunning photographs of Dr. King. Although delivered on 28 August 1963 at the Lincoln Memorial, Washington, D.C., the speech is as inspirational now as it was then. The site also contains an array of other links.

Enjoy your day on—and don't forget to bring the family.

News Release

FOR IMMEDIATE RELEASE

Contact Person: Nancy Umerang

(212) 555-9876

nancy.umerang@buttonup.com

NOCA Announces Surprise Winner of Their 2007 Integrity Award

NEW YORK, January 08, 2007. Ten years ago, Sheila McCray was a kindergarten teacher in Bend River, Texas. Today, she heads up New York–based Button Up Consulting, which provides high-level executives with critical data about their organization's resource management—from profits to personnel. What's most extraordinary about Ms. McCray's story, though, is that she just won the National Organizational Consultant Award's highest honor for integrity.

"Maybe she learned something from teaching kindergartners," joked Stanley Thorton, NOCA Director, "but she is direct and undaunted. She tells CEOs and other clients exactly what they need to hear, even if the news is bad. And, she tells them what to expect if their organization's practices get out of hand."

A hallmark of Ms. McCray's practice is the "wildfire" methodology, which exposes every element of the organization's resource management from a ten-year perspective. Yet, unlike other firms which focus chiefly on solvency issues, Ms. McCray exposes potential ethical infractions, morale and culture issues among employees, and things that might alarm investors. Ms. McCray's forecasts have been remarkably accurate; had they heeded her report warning CEFO of the potential for fraud, the company would still be flourishing today.

"My clients don't pay me to tell them that everything's nice. And, they don't expect me to be nice about it. These are full-grown professionals and they need to listen up," Ms. McCray explained. "But the reward for them is worth a small bit of worry." Ms. McCray also adds the news from her findings isn't always bad—in fact, plenty of clients get a clean bill of health and great advice about how to grow even stronger.

Sheila McCray founded Button Up Consulting in 1997 with Leslie Tannenbaum. Headquartered in New York City, they have offices in San Diego, Miami, and St. Louis. Their clients range from the M&N Corporation to the nonprofit Justice Collaboration. Ms. McCray has published numerous articles in the *Harvard Business Review*, *CEO Weekly*, and other publications. She regularly gives talks on ethical practice.

Index

O

P

About the Author

Susan F. Benjamin has brought communications issues to the nation for almost twenty years. Publications from the *Wall Street Journal* to the *Chicago Tribune* have featured Susan's novel approaches, while her opinion pieces on language-related issues have appeared in *USA Today*, the *Philadelphia Inquirer*, the *New York Daily News*, *Government Executive*, and countless others. Her other books include *Quick and Painless Business Writing* (Career Press, December 2006) and *Words at Work: Business Writing in Half the Time with Twice the Power* (Perseus, 1997).

As a speaker, Susan has appeared on CNN and National Public Radio and other broadcasts. She has trained over one hundred thousand federal and private-sector employees in numerous venues and has given keynote and other addresses. Her clients have included the Carnegie Mellon Executive Program, the National Geospacial-Intelligence Agency, Liberty Mutual Insurance Group, Fleishman Hillard International Communications, and many others.

A former professor, Susan mentored academics at Harvard University and MIT. She participated in the White House initiative on plain language under the Clinton administration, overseeing the revision of countless documents affecting millions of citizens each year. Her clients included the State Department, Department of Defense, Food and Drug Administration, as well as hundreds of private-sector organizations.

Susan's research includes assessments of organizational communication processes and studies on how language affects reader responsiveness. Articles about these findings have appeared in numerous publications, including *Scribes Legal Journal*, *Government Executive*, and *Employment Management Today*.

Susan studied philosophy and writing at Boston University and Bennington College. She received her master's in writing from Lesley College, where she worked with C. Michael Curtis, senior editor of the *Atlantic*.

Visit Susan's website at instantmarketingforalmostfree.com.